thfinder® guide

South Devon *and* Dartmoor

WALKS

Compiled by
Brian Conduit
Fully revised by
Sue Viccars

Acknowledgements
With grateful thanks to all those who kept me company during my 'ramblings'.

Text: Brian Conduit
                       Revised text for 2007 edition, Sue Viccars
Photography: Brian Conduit and Sue Viccars
Editorial: Ark Creative (UK) Ltd
Design: Ark Creative (UK) Ltd

This product includes mapping data licensed from Ordnance Survey® with the permission of the Controller of Her Majesty's Stationery Office. © Crown Copyright 2009. All rights reserved. Licence number 150002047. Ordnance Survey, the OS symbol and Pathfinder are registered trademarks and Explorer, Landranger and Outdoor Leisure are trademarks of the Ordnance Survey, the national mapping agency of Great Britain.

ISBN: 978-0-7117-0851-8

While every care has been taken to ensure the accuracy of the route directions, the publishers cannot accept responsibility for errors or omissions, or for changes in details given. The countryside is not static: hedges and fences can be removed, field boundaries can alter, footpaths can be rerouted and changes in ownership can result in the closure or diversion of some concessionary paths. Also, paths that are easy and pleasant for walking in fine conditions may become slippery, muddy and difficult in wet weather, while stepping stones across rivers and streams may become impassable.

If you find an inaccuracy in either the text or maps, please write to Crimson Publishing at the address below.

First published 1996 by Jarrold Publishing
Reprinted 1998, 2003, 2005, 2006, 2007, 2009.

This edition first published in Great Britain 2009 by Crimson Publishing,
a division of:
Crimson Business Ltd,
Westminster House, Kew Road, Richmond, Surrey, TW9 2ND

www.totalwalking.co.uk

Printed in Singapore. 7/09

A catalogue record for this book is available from the British library.

Front cover: Sidmouth, Devon
Previous page: Cockington, Devon

Contents

The National Parks and Countryside Recreation; The National Trust; The Ramblers' Association; Walkers and the Law; Countryside Access Charter; Global Positioning System (GPS); Useful Organisations; Ordnance Survey Maps

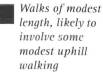

■ Short, easy walks	■ Walks of modest length, likely to involve some modest uphill walking	■ More challenging walks which may be longer and/or over more rugged terrain, often with some stiff climbs

Keymap 1

SCALE 1:277 777 or 1 INCH to about 4½ MILES 1CM to 2.7KM
KEYMAP HEIGHTS SHOWN IN FEET

PLYMOUTH to
Roscoff   6 hrs
Santander   24 hrs
(summer only)

Keymap 2

King's Nympton
Creacombe
Rackenford
Northcote Manor
King's Nympton Station
Cadbury Barton
Week
Burrington
Elstone
Lutworthy
Witheridge
Templeton Bridge
A361
Ashreigney
Chulmleigh
B3137
Calverleigh
Riddlecombe
Copy Lake
B3096
West Worlington
B3042
Nomansland
Templeton
Withleigh
Bridge Reeve
Chawleigh
Thelbridge Barton
Washford Pyne
Cruwys Morchard
Ashley
Eggesford Station
Hollocombe
Filleigh
Pennymoor
Way Village
Hele Barton
Puddington
Black Dog
Wembworthy
Eastington
Poughill
Upham
Cadeleigh
Winkleigh
Coldridge
Lapford
Lapford Cross
Woolfardisworthy
Brushford
Nymet Rowland
Morchard Bishop
Kennerleigh
B3220
Oldborough
East Village
Stockleigh English
Cheriton Fitzpaine
Broadwoodkelly
East Leigh
Morchard Road Station
Bondleigh
A3124
Newbuildings
A3072
Cadbury
Honeychurch
Zeal Monachorum
Down St Mary
Copplestone
Sandford
Upton Hellions
Stockleigh Pomeroy
North Tawton
Exbourne
Bow
Clannaborough Barton
A377
Creedy Park
Knowle
Coleford
Little Silver
Shobrooke
Efford
Thorverton
Sampford Courtenay
Nymet Tracey
CREDITON
Fordton Mill
Brampford Speke
Colebrooke
Itton
Hillerton
Yeoford
Uton
Hookway
Venny Tedburn
Newton St Cyres
Taw Green
Spreyton
B3215
South Tawton
Hittisleigh
Tedburn St Mary
Sticklepath
Belstone
Okehampton Camp
South Zeal
A30
Cheriton Bishop
Pathfinder Village
Whitestone
Cosdon Hill
Whiddon Down
Drewsteignton
Crockernwell
Longdown
Throwleigh
B3212
Ide
Alphington
Wonson
Gidleigh
Easton
Dunsford
Murchington
Shillingford St George
Dunchideock
B3206
A382
Chagford
Doccombe
Hangingstone Hill
Moretonhampstead
Bridford
Doddiscombsleigh
Frenchbeer
Kennick Reservoir
Higher Ashton
Lettaford
North Bovey
Christow
Lower Ashton
Trenchford Reservoir
Tottiford Reservoir
Sittaford Tor
Fernworthy Reservoir
13
Lustleigh
B3193
Trusham
A38
A380
DARTMOOR
Grimspound
Manaton
Hennock
Hameldown Tor
Bovey Tracey
Chudleigh
B3344
Rough Tor
Postbridge
FOREST
Ashcombe
Bellever
Cator Court
Widecombe in the Moor
Brimley
Haytor Vale
Chudleigh Knighton
Heathfield
Ideford
Luton
B3192
Two Bridges
HM Prison
Babeny
B3387
Rippon
Ilsington
Coldeast
Liverton
3
Bishopsteignton
26
B3357
Ponsworthy
21
Sigford
Exeter Cross
Teigngrace
Kingsteignton
Princetown
West Dart River
Dartmeet
Buckland in the Moor
NEWTON ABBOT
Bickington
R. TEIGN
Hexworthy
2
Caton
A383
Netherton
Combeinteignhead
Whiteworks
Venford Reservoir
16
East Ogwell
West Ogwell
Stokeinteignhead
Haccombe
Burrator Reservoir
28
ASHBURTON
Woodland
Abbotskerswell
Cater's Beam
Ryder's Hill
Holne
Scorriton
Denbury
Kingskerswell
Coffinswell
Daccombe
Sheepstor
Forder Green
Torbryan
North Whilborough
Buckfast
Abbey
Landscove
Ipplepen
Barton
BUCKFASTLEIGH
Woolston Green
Broadhempston
A381
Avon Dam Reservoir
Dean
Staverton
Compton
Shiphay
Shell Top
Dean Prior
A384
Dartington
Dartington Hall
Littlehempston
Marldon
1
Ugborough Moor
Harbourneford
Didworthy
Rattery
Berry Pomeroy
Blagdon
Lee Moor
A385
Tigley
Cott
Castle
South Brent
TOTNES
Corntwood
Drakeland Corner
Lutton
Harford
Ugborough Beacon
Avonwick
Bulsford
Collaton St Mary
PAIGNTON
Goodrington
Bittaford
Lincombe
Harberton
Stoke Gabriel
IVYBRIDGE
B3213
Ashprington
A3022

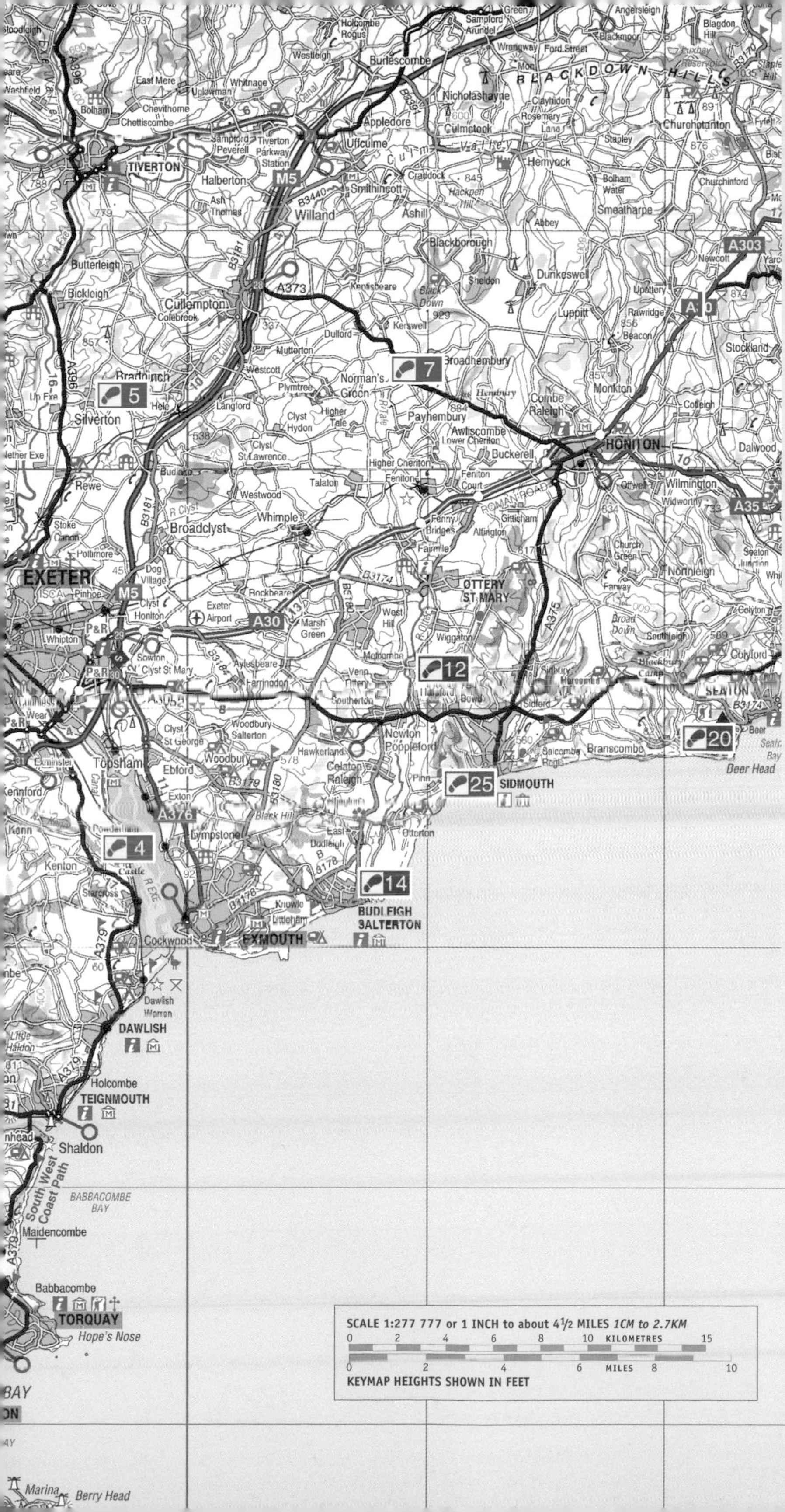

BLACKDOWN HILLS

TIVERTON

EXETER

HONITON

OTTERY ST MARY

SEATON

SIDMOUTH

BUDLEIGH SALTERTON

EXMOUTH

DAWLISH

TEIGNMOUTH

Shaldon

BABBACOMBE BAY

Maidencombe

Babbacombe

TORQUAY

Hope's Nose

Berry Head

South West Coast Path

SCALE 1:277 777 or 1 INCH to about 4½ MILES *1CM to 2.7KM*

| 0 | 2 | 4 | 6 | 8 | 10 | KILOMETRES | 15 |

| 0 | 2 | 4 | 6 | MILES | 8 | 10 |

KEYMAP HEIGHTS SHOWN IN FEET

Walk	Page	Start	Nat. Grid Reference	Distance	Time	Highest Point
Ashburton & Whiddon Scrubbs	49	Ashburton	SX 756698	5½ miles (8.75km)	3hrs	986ft (210m)
Beer and Branscombe	59	Beer	SY 228889	6½ miles (10.5km)	3½hrs	459ft (140m)
Bench Tor	16	Venford Reservoir	SX 685713	2½ miles (4km)	1½hrs	1017ft (310m)
Bolt Head and Salcombe Estuary	56	North Sands, Salcombe	SX 730382	6 miles (9.5km)	3½hrs	427ft (130m)
Brixham and Churston Point	46	Brixham	SX 926563	6 miles (9.5km)	3hrs	164ft (50m)
Broadhembury	26	Broadhembury	ST 102047	5 miles (8km)	2½hrs	886ft (270m)
Buckfastleigh Moor	86	Holne	SX 706696	10 miles (16km)	6hrs	1690ft (515m)
Cockington Valley	14	Cockington	SX 895638	3 miles (4.75km)	1½hrs	328ft (100m)
Dart Estuary and Dartmouth Castle	32	Little Dartmouth	SX 874492	3½ miles (5.5km)	2hrs	394ft (120m)
Dittisham, Cornworthy and Tuckenhay	82	Dittisham	SX 865551	9½ miles (15.25km)	5hrs	427ft (130m)
Exe Estuary and Exminster Marshes	20	Powderham church	SX 974845	5½ miles (8.75km)	2½hrs	16ft (5m)
Gara Rock and Portlemouth Down	34	Mill Bay	SX 743381	3½ miles (5.5km)	2hrs	328ft (100m)
Loddiswell and the Avon Valley Woods	29	Loddiswell	SX 720486	5½ miles (8.75km)	3hrs	328ft (100m)
Otter Estuary, East Budleigh and Otterton	43	Budleigh Salterton	SY 072820	6½ miles (10.5km)	3½hrs	131ft (40m)
Prawle Point and Woodcombe Point	52	Prawle Point	SX 775354	5½ miles (8.75km)	3hrs	394ft (120m)
Princetown, Dartmoor Railway and Leather Tor	78	Princetown	SX 591735	10 miles (16km)	5hrs	1477ft (450m)
Rippon Tor, Pil Tor and Buckland Beacon	62	Cold East Cross	SX 741743	6½ miles (10.5km)	3½hrs	1214ft (370m)
Sidmouth, Salcombe Regis and Weston Combe	74	Sidmouth	SY 126872	8 miles (12.75km)	4hrs	558ft (170m)
Silverton and Christ Cross	22	Silverton	SS 955028	4½ miles (7.25km)	2½hrs	853ft (260m)
Start Point and Hallsands	54	Start Point	SX 821375	6½ miles (10.5km)	3½hrs	394ft (120m)
Stover Country Park and the River Teign	18	Stover Country Park	SX 833748	5 miles (8km)	2½hrs	66ft (20m)
Three Reservoirs Walk	40	Bullaton Cross picnic site	SX 805824	6 miles (9.5km)	3hrs	919ft (280m)
Torcross, Slapton Ley and Stokenham	65	Torcross	SX 824423	7 miles (11.25km)	3½hrs	328ft (100m)
Venn Ottery Common	38	Tipton St John	SY 091917	5 miles (8km)	2½hrs	263ft (80m)
Vixen Tor and Pew Tor	24	west of Merrivale Bridge	SX 539750	4 miles (6.5km)	2hrs	1050ft (320m)
Widgery Cross and Great Links Tor	68	Car park off A386	SX 525854	6½ miles (10.5km)	3½hrs	1925ft (586m)
Yealm Estuary	36	Noss Mayo	SX 546474	4½ miles (7.25km)	2½hrs	328ft (100m)
Yes Tor and High Willhays	71	Okehampton Moor Gate	SX 592932	6 miles (9.5km)	3½hrs	2039ft (621m)

After walking through a thickly wooded valley, the final part of the route offers fine views over the southern fringes of Dartmoor.

An energetic and highly scenic route that includes two attractive villages, a Norman church, fine coastal woodlands and some superb cliff walking.

On this walk you get one of the finest views over Dartmoor for very little effort.

A rugged but easy section of coastline is followed at the end by a dramatic walk along the western side of the estuary.

The walk takes you along the stretch of coast to the east of the fishing town of Brixham, on the fringes of Torbay.

From a picturesque thatched village with a fine medieval church follow the route round the edge of a typical, well-wooded Devonian combe.

Much of this challenging walk is across pathless moorland and the route is best left for fine weather when the extensive views can be appreciated to the full.

A short walk from an idyllic village and through a lovely secluded valley, all within a short distance of the seafront at Torquay.

Expect quite a lot of climbing on this short walk that takes in a late medieval castle and offers spectacular views across the estuary.

A fairly tortuous route with some steep climbs and muddy and overgrown paths in places, but varied and absorbing also, with some superb views.

A fresh, open walk across marshes and by a canal and river estuary, but after rain some muddy stretches can be expected.

A gentle ascent along a beautiful wooded track is followed by a splendid coastal walk with fine views across the Salcombe estuary.

A delightful and relaxing ramble through steep sided riverside woodlands is the highlight of this walk.

The route starts at a small seaside resort by an estuary and explores an attractive river valley, taking in two villages and passing a restored mill.

Pass the most southerly point on the South Devon coast on a walk which runs along one of its most spectacular stretches.

A lengthy but not strenuous walk which offers the experience of Dartmoor at its wildest and bleakest.

Five tors are climbed on this walk, all of them magnificent viewpoints, and there is also the opportunity to take in an idyllic, tucked away thatched hamlet.

There are a number of stiff climbs, especially along the switchback cliffs on the final part of the walk, but the outstanding views more than compensate.

Enjoy fine views looking across to Dartmoor, the Blackdown Hills and even distant Exmoor on both the ascent and descent.

From the headland at the start, the views encompass a long stretch of coast from Torbay to the Salcombe estuary.

A circuit of a lake, plus woodland, meadow and riverside walking, following an easy and well-waymarked trail.

Three reservoirs on the eastern fringes of Dartmoor are linked by this walk, much of which is through conifer woodland.

Memories of a Second World War disaster, a nature reserve based around a lagoon, and a splendid medieval church provide plenty of interest and variety.

This walk climbs out of the valley on to one of the remaining expanses of open heathland in south east Devon.

Boggy conditions can be expected at times on this fine scenic walk across open moorland that takes in several tors.

The whole of this walk, which involves one steep climb, is across open moorland and the views, especially over West Devon, are outstanding.

There could hardly be a flatter or easier coastal walk in South Devon as it follows a carriage drive laid out by a local Victorian land owner.

The two highest points in southern England offer the most superb and extensive views.

At-a-glance...

Introduction to
South Devon and Dartmoor

The aim of this walking guide is to extend the scope of the existing *Pathfinder Guide to Dartmoor*. It includes some more walks within the Dartmoor National Park but adds routes in the other parts of South Devon – on the hills and in the river valleys of the South Hams and south east Devon, and especially along the spectacular coastline, the jewel of the region – thus increasing the choice and variety.

At the crossroads of South Devon is Exeter, ancient Roman settlement, medieval cathedral city and county town. To the west lies the great granite massif of Dartmoor, while to the south east, south and south west the long line of the coast stretches from Beer near the Dorset border to Plymouth on the fringes of Cornwall. The transition from coast to moor is quite a dramatic and sudden one. A short journey northwards from Torquay – where in the almost subtropical conditions palm trees grow on the promenade – subjects you to one of the most abrupt changes of scenery likely to be encountered anywhere in this country. A few miles in distance and a few hundred feet in height transports you to the last great wilderness in southern England, the open and majestic terrain of Dartmoor, parts of which are as bleak and remote as anywhere in the wildest regions of the northern Pennines.

Dartmoor

As well as being justifiably acclaimed as the last great wilderness in southern England, Dartmoor also contains the highest land in England south of the Pennines. Main roads across the moor are relatively few and side roads and country lanes are often narrower than in other parts of the country – as many an exasperated holiday motorist is able to testify. The few towns and villages are mostly concentrated around the edge of the moor, particularly in the river valleys and the gentler country on the south and east, while on the wilder expanses of the north and west they are largely non-existent.

The central heartland of the open moor is surrounded by rolling downs, thickly wooded gorges and pleasant river valleys with picture postcard villages of thatch and granite. The valleys are benign and welcoming but in contrast the moors can be most inhospitable, even dangerous, and as such need to be treated with respect and caution. Route finding across these bare expanses can be difficult as paths tend to peter out, and the lack of easily identifiable landmarks means it is easy for walkers to get lost, especially in misty conditions. But these austere, sweeping moorlands, their hilltops studded with the ubiquitous granite tors – the most characteristic element of the Dartmoor landscape – are endowed with a haunting and melancholic beauty that is undeniably appealing.

From the largely uninhabited central wilderness rise Dartmoor's rivers – the Lyd, Tavy, Meavy, Walkham, Plym, Yealm, Erme, Avon, East and West Dart, Bovey, Teign, Taw and Okement – all of which, except the last two, flow southwards to the English Channel. The reasons for the flow of the rivers and for the wilder scenery being in the north and west lie in the geology and climate of the region. Dartmoor is a great mass of granite rising above the surrounding farmlands like a brooding giant. Immense primeval earth movements tilted this mass towards the south and east, which explains why the highest (and wettest) land is in the north and west and why the majority of the rivers flow southwards. The granite core is edged with areas of softer rocks – slates, shales, limestone and sandstone – and where the rivers leave the harder granite and reach these softer rocks, they have sometimes cut deep narrow ravines, such as the gorges of the Dart, Teign and Lyd.

The tors are remnants of hard masses of granite, moulded into their present shapes by millions of years of weathering. The most conspicuous of these – Haytor Rocks, Hound Tor, Vixen Tor – are not only impressive in themselves but act as vital landmarks for walkers in an otherwise often featureless landscape. Historical remains from all ages lie scattered over Dartmoor, evidence both of continuous occupation and of the long history of human exploitation of the moor. Few areas of Britain have a higher concentration of prehistoric monuments and these include burial chambers, avenues, standing stones, hut circles and hill forts. The discovery of tin around the middle of the 12th century led to the growth of a flourishing tin-mining industry throughout the Middle Ages and Tudor period, and its relics provide a fertile field for those interested in industrial archaeology.

Later in the 19th century there was a great demand for Dartmoor granite and quarrying boomed. First tramways and later railways were constructed across the moor to transport the granite down to the coast and many of these now disused tracks make excellent, clearly defined walking routes. Demand for water from Plymouth and the fast-growing holiday resorts of Torbay led to the construction of reservoirs on the moor. Since the 1870s the army has used a large part of northern Dartmoor for military training purposes. During the 20th century a number of conifer plantations have been established. All these developments have left their mark on the present-day landscape of Dartmoor and, like the disused railway tracks and earlier routeways, water board and forestry tracks and army roads – which some purists decry – can be used by walkers to aid navigation and provide relatively easy, well-

Dartmouth Castle

surfaced routes. The long history of mineral working on Dartmoor is over and the mainstay of the economy nowadays, as with the rest of South Devon, is tourism. As a recognition of its immense landscape value and recreational role, Dartmoor was designated one of Britain's national parks in 1951.

South Devon

Spreading out like a fan to the south and south east of Dartmoor is a landscape that is typically Devonian, a region of soft, rolling, well-wooded hills, lush pastures and deep river valleys leading on to long, winding estuaries and the coast. The area immediately to the south, bounded by the Tamar in the west and Dart in the east and forming a triangular-shaped wedge jutting out into the Channel, is the South Hams. This is rich farming country dotted with attractive villages, imposing medieval churches and fine old towns such as Totnes, Dartmouth and Kingsbridge. The chief glory of the South Hams is its coastline, broken up by the rias or long, deep estuaries of the Tamar, the various inlets of the Salcombe estuary, Avon, Erme and Dart. These sheltered estuaries provided good harbours and during the Middle Ages Plymouth and Dartmouth developed into major ports and naval bases, a role that the former, the largest city in Devon, has maintained. During the Second World War many of the quiet estuaries and now small ports, fishing villages and genteel resorts along this coast had a new lease of life as they played a vital role in the build-up to the D-Day landings, providing a base for thousands of American forces.

East of the Dart lies Torbay and the start of the popular holiday coast that reaches to the Dorset border. It was during the Napoleonic Wars, when

Branscombe church

the English aristocracy were cut off from their usual continental haunts, that this area first became popular and many of the resorts – Torquay, Teignmouth, Exmouth and Sidmouth – still retain some of their graceful Regency architecture. The coming of the railways considerably added to the number of visitors, attracted by the combination of a mild and sunny climate, good sandy beaches and outstanding scenery. Nowadays it is still one of the most popular holiday destinations in Britain, made even more accessible by the M5 motorway.

From Torbay eastwards across the Teign and Exe estuaries to Sidmouth and beyond there are some impressive stretches of dark red sandstone cliffs that provide excellent and challenging walking. At Beer Head the red sandstone gives way to gleaming white chalk, heralding the start of the Dorset coast. Inland there is pleasant countryside in the two main river valleys of the Otter and Sid, with more attractive villages of thatched cottages and imposing churches and some surviving areas of rough heathland standing above the neat and orderly farmland. In 2001 the 95 mile (155km) stretch of coastline from Exmouth in Devon to Old Harry Rocks in Dorset was designated 'the Jurassic Coast', England's first World Heritage Site, on account of its fantastic geological history.

Walking in the Area

For most walkers the primary attractions in South Devon and Dartmoor are the coast and moor, and the majority of the walks which we feature in this book concentrate on those two areas. In addition, the good walking country in the hills and valleys of the South Hams and south east Devon that lie between has not been ignored. Rights of way throughout the area are generally well-waymarked, except on the central heartland of Dartmoor where they are not always visible on the ground. Here you'll find that routes either strike out across the open moor or capitalise on the many disused, former mining and quarrying tracks. The whole length of the coastline is traversed by the South West Coast Path national trail and presents no real route-finding difficulties, but some of the lesser used paths in the lush country between the coast and moor may well become overgrown during the summer months.

With a choice of open moorland, an often dramatic coastline, wooded river valleys, estuaries and creeks, plus picturesque thatched villages with pubs and tea shops dispensing the traditional local delicacies of pasties, cider and cream teas, the walker in South Devon really is in a position to enjoy the best of all worlds.

With the introduction of '**gps enabled**' walks, you will see that this book now includes a list of waypoints alongside the description of the walk. We have included these so that you can enjoy the full benefits of gps should you wish to. Gps is an amazingly useful and entertaining navigational aid, and you do not need to be computer literate to enjoy it.

GPS waypoint co-ordinates add value to your walk. You will now have the extra advantage of introducing 'direction' into your walking which will enhance your leisure walking and make it safer. Use of a gps brings greater confidence and security and you will find you cover ground a lot faster should you need to.

For more detailed information on using your gps, a *Pathfinder Guide* introducing you to gps and digital mapping is now available. *GPS for Walkers*, written by experienced gps teacher and navigation trainer Clive Thomas, is available in bookshops (ISBN 978-0-7117-4445-5) or order online at www.totalwalking.co.uk

Cockington Valley

		GPS waypoints	
Start	Cockington		SX 894 638
Distance	3 miles (4.75km)	Ⓐ	SX 886 639
Approximate time	1½ hours	Ⓑ	SX 888 636
Parking	Cockington	Ⓒ	SX 889 638
Refreshments	Pub and tearooms at Cockington, café at Cockington Court	Ⓓ	SX 892 637
		Ⓔ	SX 889 634
Ordnance Survey maps	Landranger 202 (Torbay & South Dartmoor), Explorers OL20 (South Devon) and 110 (Torquay & Dawlish)	Ⓕ	SX 896 635

Despite being almost engulfed by the suburban expansion of Torbay, the secluded and well-wooded Cockington valley has survived untouched as a little enclave of traditional, rural England complete with thatched village, meadows, woods and parkland. It has now been designated a country park and this short walk, which starts from the visitor centre, explores the many facets of this unusual, fascinating and undeniably beautiful valley.

Thatched and colour-washed cottages, forge, mill with water wheel, pub, cricket field, church and manor house, all tucked away in a tranquil and wooded valley, make Cockington the archetypal English village of calendars and picture postcards. Its proximity to Torquay – only 1 mile (1.6km) from the seafront – makes it inevitably popular with holidaymakers, and the amenities that it offers to visitors – gift shops, Devon cream teas and horse-drawn open carriage rides around the village – only add to the quaintness of the scene. The church and manor house are a short distance from the village centre and these will be passed later on during the walk.

🖉 Begin by turning right out of the visitor centre car park along the lane, passing to the right of the Drum Inn. This only dates from the 1930s but was designed by Sir Edwin Lutyens to harmonise with its 'olde-world' surroundings. At a public footpath sign to 'Marldon via Bewhay Lane', turn left along an enclosed, sunken track which heads uphill and emerges into more open country, later becoming a hedge-lined path. Ignore a waymarked track left. At the 'Horse Riding Route' sign, follow the path around in a complete U-turn Ⓐ. Go through a gate and turn right to continue, between a fence on the left and hedge on the right, above the head of the valley, with fine views to the left of Cockington Court and the church below, and Torquay and the coast on the skyline beyond.

Keep along this undulating path to where it bends first to the left and then sharply to the right. At this point Ⓑ keep ahead down steps to a public footpath sign for Cockington

Court a few yards ahead, and turn left over a stile. Follow the narrow path gently downhill by a fence on the left, entering woodland and winding down to a stile. Climb the stile and a few yards ahead turn right **C** over another stile on to a tarmac path through the grounds of Cockington Court, passing between the house on the left and church on the right, side by side in the traditional English manner. The 16th-century manor house, set amid lovely rolling parkland, now houses a craft centre and tearoom. The simple but attractive church, with a low west tower, is of Norman origin. Both buildings are in perfect harmony with their surroundings.

In front of the house turn right along the broad tarmac drive running through the park beside the cricket field on the left – watch out for horse-drawn carriages – and, at a fork, take the right hand track **D**, signposted 'Gamekeepers Cottage, The Lakes, Woodland Walk'. The track bears to the right, goes through a cutting and under a bridge. At the next fork continue along the right hand track through colourful and attractive gardens. Pass to the right of the thatched Gamekeepers Cottage and then bear right to continue uphill, signed Warren Barn – now the track will have become rough – along the right, inside edge of Manscombe Plantation.

At a footpath junction in front of Warren Barn turn left **E**, doubling back through the wood. The path passes a green marker post and starts to descend. At the next fork look out for where a

Cockington church

green marker post directs you to continue along the right-hand, upper path. This is a most attractive stretch of the walk and the earlier track can be seen below. Keep ahead all the while, passing round two wooden barriers and crossing a path. At a T-junction of paths at the end of the wood turn left and head steeply downhill via a flight of steps to a tarmac path. Turn sharp right and then left to rejoin the main tarmac drive by one of the small lakes that are a feature of the grounds. Turn sharp right, continue downhill, passing through a Gothic gateway, to a road. Turn left **F** and follow it back to the centre of Cockington village. ●

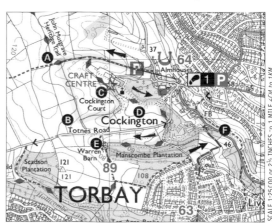

Bench Tor

		GPS waypoints
Start	Venford Reservoir. Car park on west side of dam	SX 685 712
Distance	2½ miles (4km)	Ⓐ SX 687 711
Approximate time	1½ hours	Ⓑ SX 695 713
Parking	Venford Reservoir	Ⓒ SX 691 716
Refreshments	None	
Ordnance Survey maps	Landranger 202 (Torbay & South Dartmoor), Explorer OL28 (Dartmoor)	

There can be few walks of this modest length that offer such outstanding views and are more enjoyable than this one. From Venford Reservoir you take a clear and easy woodland path that follows the curve of the river above the thickly wooded Dart gorge, eventually climbing steadily to the magnificent viewpoint of Bench Tor 312m (1025ft). From here it is a gentle descent back to the start. Although a short and easy walk, it is advisable not to attempt it in misty weather as the final section could be difficult without the landmark of the reservoir as a guide.

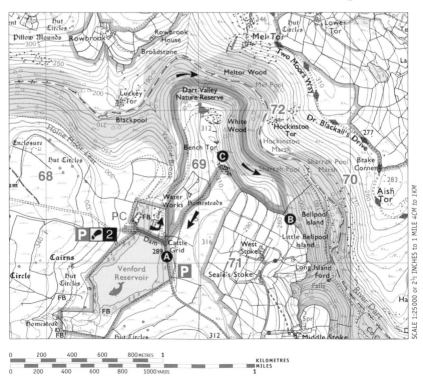

SCALE 1:25000 or 2½ INCHES to 1 MILE 4CM to 1KM

```
0    200   400   600   800 METRES  1
0    200   400   600   800   1000 YARDS
                                          KILOMETRES
                                          MILES
                                          1
```

A panoramic view over Dartmoor from Bench Tor

From the car park head down to the road to cross the dam. On the other side climb a low embankment and then turn left **Ⓐ** alongside railings which border woodland that surrounds a water treatment works. Where the railings turn left, bear left and head downhill across grass to join a path which runs just above Venford Brook.

Bear right along this most attractive path – flat, grassy and well constructed. Initially it keeps above the brook but later curves right through steep-sided, rocky woodland, giving excellent views through the trees of the thickly wooded Dart gorge. The river is only occasionally glimpsed below but can always be heard. Later the path climbs steadily and emerges from the trees to give another superb view across the Dart valley to the open moor. On reaching a gate, do not go through it but turn right **Ⓑ** and head uphill, by a wall on the left. Where the wall bears left, keep straight ahead to Bench Tor, bearing right to the highest of the collection of rocks **Ⓒ** in order to enjoy one of the finest panoramic views over Dartmoor.

Several worn, grassy paths lead from Bench Tor down to the reservoir below; turn left and make your way down, heading for the centre of the reservoir, flanked by conifers. The gentle, almost unnoticeable descent should bring you out on to the road by the end of the dam. Turn right over the dam to return to the starting point. ●

Stover Country Park and the River Teign

Start	Stover Country Park		GPS waypoints
Distance	5 miles (8km)		✐ SX 832 749
Approximate time	2 hours		Ⓐ SX 836 751
Parking	Stover Country Park		Ⓑ SX 843 749
Refreshments	None		Ⓒ SX 847 747
Ordnance Survey maps	Landranger 202 (Torbay & South Devon), Explorer 110 (Torquay & Dawlish)		Ⓓ SX 854 743
			Ⓔ SX 848 741

This is an entirely flat walk – a rarity in South Devon. It starts in the wooded surroundings of Stover Country Park, encircles a lake and includes a pleasant stretch of riverside walking beside the Teign. In addition it is an easy walk to follow, well-waymarked all the way with 'Templer Way, Heritage Trail' signs.

During the 18th century James Templer, a local man, made a fortune from the exploitation of the granite and ball clay resources of Dartmoor, and used some of his wealth to build a grand house surrounded by landscaped parkland in the Teign valley. The house is now a girls' school and the grounds form Stover Country Park. The route by which Templer and his successors brought granite down from Haytor and transported ball clay down the Stover Canal to the Teign estuary and the sea, is now a waymarked trail, the Templer Way. The Templer Way Heritage Trail is a shorter circular walk that includes the Country Park, River Teign and Stover Canal.

✐ Start at the information centre and take the track that passes to the left of it into the trees, signed to the Templer Way. Turn right at a T-junction, by a notice board, and the track curves left to the lake which

was created by James Templer around 1765 as part of the landscaped grounds of Stover House. Turn left over a footbridge and follow a tree-lined path around Stover Lake. There are attractive views from here across the water, with waterlilies on the surface and rhododendron bushes fringing the edges of the lake. Keep beside the water, curving right all the while and crossing several footbridges. Eventually turn right over a footbridge at the eastern end of the lake to reach a notice board which indicates the start of the Heritage Trail Ⓐ. Turn left, in the direction of the 'Templer Way, Heritage Trail, and Ventiford', keeping next to a channel on the left.

At the end of the channel, by a cascade, turn right along a path that winds through woodland, later passing through some rather gloomy conifers, and go through a gate on to the road and turn right. After a few

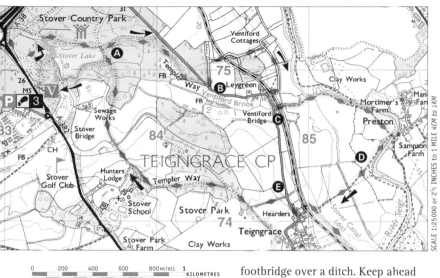

SCALE 1:25000 or 2½ INCHES to 1 MILE 4CM to 1KM

yards turn left **B**, along Summer Lane, and follow it around a right-hand bend and over a railway bridge. In front of cottages turn right and the lane bends right under another railway bridge to rejoin the road. Turn left over Ventiford Bridge and immediately turn left **C** along a track, by a brook on the left. Pass under the railway again, go through a kissing-gate and take the path ahead, which initially keeps along the left edge of a field and later heads across to the River Teign. Go through a kissing-gate and continue along the edge of meadows beside the tree-lined riverbank. This is a most attractive part of the walk with fine views to the right across the fields to the southern slopes of Dartmoor, with Haytor prominent on the skyline.

Follow the river around a right-hand curve, passing two bridges over the river and keeping along the riverbank all the time. Look out for a Templer Way post, which directs you to the right **D**, across a meadow, to a kissing-gate. Go through, continue across the meadow, go through another kissing-gate and cross a

footbridge over a ditch. Keep ahead to a T-junction of paths, turn right and shortly turn left to cross Teigngrace Locks Bridge over the disused Stover Canal, built by the second James Templer to transport ball clay. It ran for two miles (3.25km) from Ventiford to the Teign estuary.

Continue over the railway line and along a drive to a road. Turn right and at a Templer Way post, turn left **E** to go through two gates in quick succession – one metal and one wooden. Follow a path across meadows and the tower of Teigngrace church is seen to the left. This too was built by James Templer II, in 1786. Go through a kissing-gate on to a track and turn right, and you will shortly enter woodland. The track emerges from the trees to reach a fork; continue along the right-hand track, between a hedge on the right and woodland on the left, descending into more open country and crossing a bridge.

Pass back into woodland again and just before reaching a footbridge by the Heritage Trail starting point **A**, turn left to complete the circuit of Stover Lake. Cross a footbridge and turn right. At the next footbridge turn left and retrace your steps to the start. ●

Exe Estuary and Exminster Marshes

		GPS waypoints
Start	Powderham church	
Distance	5½ miles (8.75km)	SX 972 844
Approximate time	2½ hours	Ⓐ SX 963 861
Parking	Roadside parking spaces by Powderham church	Ⓑ SX 954 872 Ⓒ SX 962 879
Refreshments	Turf Hotel by canal and estuary	
Ordnance Survey maps	Landranger 192 (Exeter & Sidmouth), Explorer 110 (Torquay & Dawlish)	

Wide views and fresh, invigorating breezes accompany this flat and easy walk along the west bank of the Exe estuary and across the Exminster marshes (RSPB reserve), which are a haven for wildlife. The return leg uses the towpath of the Exeter Canal, which runs parallel to the river before emptying into it. The section across the marshes is likely to be muddy or have surface water after wet weather.

📷 Walk down the lane to the left of Powderham church, a fine, red sandstone, mainly 13th-century building. As the lane bends right turn left at a public footpath sign along a track that leads off from the road below a railway embankment on the right. Turn right through a metal kissing-gate to cross the railway line

View from the towpath of the Exeter Canal

– take care here – and turn left to continue beside the sea wall above the estuary. All around there are wide views: to the right across the Exe, to the left across meadows to low wooded hills, and ahead the buildings of Exeter can be seen in the distance.

The track swings right through a kissing-gate and over a stile to pass to the left of the Turf Hotel, where the Exeter Canal empties into the river. This was the first major canal in the country, originally built in the 16th century to link Exeter with Topsham. The canal was later extended and improved, and converted into a ship canal, the oldest in Britain. At a public footpath sign turn left Ⓐ down to cross a footbridge over a channel. Climb a stile and then continue diagonally right across a low-lying meadow.

On the far side climb two stiles and the intervening footbridge. Follow the path to the left and after crossing a footbridge, the path bends right to continue by a railway embankment on the left. Go through a series of kissing-gates to reach a tarmac track and turn right along it to reach a lane **B**.

Turn right and walk along the lane as far as a right-hand bend and at a public footpath sign keep ahead to cross two footbridges. Continue across meadows, over a succession of footbridges crossing channels, eventually going through a kissing-gate and heading up to the canal towpath **C**. Ahead across the river is historic Topsham, Exeter's port in Roman times. Turn right along the towpath (keeping an eye out for cyclists) and continue to the Turf Hotel **A**. The Turf Lock was built in 1827. From here retrace your steps to the start. ●

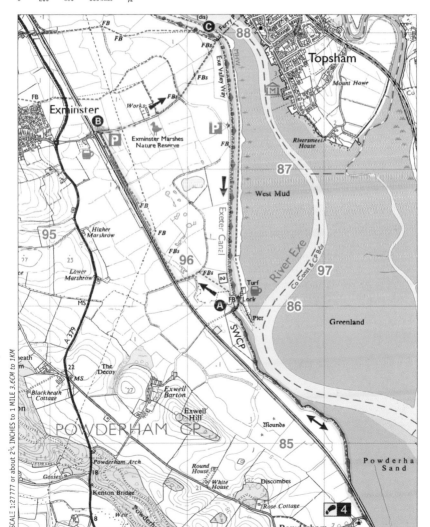

Silverton and Christ Cross

		GPS waypoints
Start	Silverton	🥾 SS 955 028
Distance	4½ miles (7.25km)	Ⓐ SS 956 031
Approximate time	2½ hours	Ⓑ SS 961 042
Parking	Silverton	Ⓒ SS 966 050
Refreshments	Pubs at Silverton	Ⓓ SS 973 044
Ordnance Survey maps	Landranger 192 (Exeter & Sidmouth), Explorer 114 (Exeter & the Exe Valley)	Ⓔ SS 963 034

From Silverton a steady uphill climb along a mixture of tracks, field paths and quiet lanes, leads up to the superb viewpoint of Christ Cross where on a clear day the view extends right across mid Devon to the distant outline of Exmoor. On the gradual descent equally outstanding views open up to the Black Down Hills and across the Exe valley to Dartmoor. The walk is well-waymarked and easy to follow but expect some permanently muddy sections; good boots are essential.

Despite some modern housing and proximity to Exeter and the M5, Silverton retains a remote, sleepy and pleasantly old-fashioned atmosphere, complete with a number of attractive thatched cottages. The battlemented exterior of the mainly 15th-century church gives it (the building) a sturdy and imposing appearance.

🥾 The walk starts in the village centre by the war memorial. Walk up Fore Street, a picturesque mixture of brick and colour-washed houses and cottages – some thatched – and, opposite the Lamb Inn, turn right Ⓐ along Parsonage Lane beside the redbrick Methodist church. At the end of the lane bear right to continue along a tarmac path by a new housing area, cross a road and keep ahead along an enclosed, hedge-lined tarmac track.

The track heads steadily uphill and where the tarmac finishes, turn left over a stile, at a public footpath sign, and continue uphill along the right edge of a field. Just before reaching the top, where the field edge begins to curve left, turn right through a hedge gap to climb a stile and continue steadily uphill along the right-hand edge of the field, between a wire fence on the left and hedge on the right. The path, which is narrow, later descends slightly to a stile. Climb this on to a lane Ⓑ, turn right and then follow the lane uphill for ¾ mile (1.2km) to the junction of lanes at Christ Cross Ⓒ. This is a grand viewpoint, especially looking northwards across the rolling country of mid Devon to Exmoor on the horizon.

At the junction, turn sharp right along a narrow, enclosed lane heading gently downhill. Ahead are views towards the coast. Gaps in the hedges on both sides reveal fine views: to the left, towards the Black

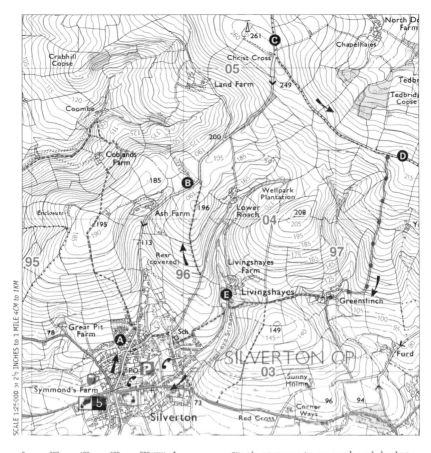

Down Hills and Somerset, and to the right over the Exe valley to the edge of Dartmoor.

Where the lane begins to ascend slightly, turn right **D** at a 'Circular Walk' post, along an enclosed track which could be muddy after rain and overgrown in summer. Follow it steadily downhill for just over ½ mile (800m), eventually bending right and continuing down to Greenshill Barton Farm. At the farm entrance bear left along a track. Where the track bears sharp left and becomes tarmac keep straight ahead along another track – there is a public footpath sign here – passing to the right of houses Negotiate a very muddy stretch, beyond which the track narrows to an enclosed, hedge- and tree-lined path. Where the path ends turn left over a stile. Turn right and continue downhill towards Silverton, by the right edge of a sloping field. Climb a stile in the field corner and continue down an enclosed path to a tarmac lane. Turn left **E** along the lane and after a few yards turn right over a stile, at a 'Circular Walk' waymark. Bear left, head uphill across a field to join the hedge on the right, and climb a stile in the field corner. Keep ahead to climb another stile. Turn left along a path between two fences and follow this around a right-hand bend and on to a road. Turn left along the road through a modern housing area on the edge of Silverton, bending right to a T-junction. Turn right to return to the village centre. ●

Vixen Tor and Pew Tor

Start	Car park ¾ mile (1.2km) west of Merrivale Bridge on B3357. First car park on right past Merrivale Bridge and quarry entrance if coming from the east; second on the left after the large car park on the right if coming from the west
Distance	4 miles (6.5km)
Approximate time	2 hours
Parking	Car park west of Merrivale Bridge
Refreshments	None
Ordnance Survey maps	Landranger 201 (Plymouth & Launceston), Explorer OL28 (Dartmoor)

GPS waypoints

- ⬤ SX 540 749
- Ⓐ SX 541 743
- Ⓑ SX 535 734
- Ⓒ SX 532 734
- Ⓓ SX 526 732
- Ⓔ SX 526 738
- Ⓕ SX 532 742
- Ⓖ SX 534 751

The 28m (90ft) Vixen Tor is one of the most distinctive, as well as the tallest, of the tors on Dartmoor. The walk begins by heading across open moorland to the tor and continues above the western side of the attractive Walkham valley before climbing to the viewpoint of Pew Tor. The route returns across the open expanses of Whitchurch Common, passing the isolated landmark of Windy Cross. All the way there are extensive views across moorland to the encircling tors but there is some rough walking in places and expect some boggy sections after rain.

⬤ Begin by crossing the road and heading straight across the open moor, negotiating boulders, towards the prominent outline of Vixen Tor. Cross a leat, continue – this part is likely to be boggy – and at a wall in front of the tor turn right Ⓐ. Head gently downhill, bending left. Keep near the wall to cross the stream on granite boulders. Continue by the wall on the left, curving right and heading uphill to make your way through an area of gorse, rocks and stunted trees to the left of Heckwood Tor. To the left are fine views over the Walkham valley, ahead the tower of Sampford Spiney church can be seen, and as the path bears right Pew Tor comes into view.

Where the wall bends left, keep ahead along the path and, where this curves left shortly afterwards, turn right Ⓑ on to a path that soon bends right and climbs up to Pew Tor Ⓒ, where the magnificent panoramic views include Plymouth Sound.

Continue over the tor, keep on downhill to pass to the left of a disused quarry then follow a grassy path that bears left and heads gently downhill. At the bottom bear left to continue between gorse bushes, alongside a leat on the right. Where the leat runs parallel to a lane, cross the water Ⓓ. Turn sharp right along this narrow lane to where it bends sharp left. Turn right Ⓔ to follow a

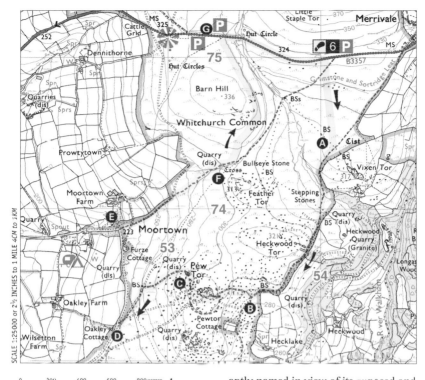

path gently uphill, keeping parallel to a wall on the left. After the wall turns away left, continue straight ahead across gorse-strewn moorland, fording a leat on a track **F** and bearing slightly right to follow it to Windy Cross. From this ancient landmark,

The isolated Windy Cross – a useful landmark

aptly named in view of its exposed and isolated location, there are wide views all around: Vixen Tor, the Walkham valley and King's Tor are to the right and ahead the view is dominated by Cox Tor and Great Staple Tor. Continue beside the leat across Whitchurch Common. Where the leat bears away right keep ahead by a stream to reach the B3357 opposite a car park **G**. Turn right along it to the next car park which is the starting point. ●

Broadhembury

Start	Broadhembury		GPS waypoints
Distance	5 miles (8km)		🥾 ST 101 047
Approximate time	2½ hours		Ⓐ ST 117 053
Parking	In the village square at Broadhembury		Ⓑ ST 115 066
			Ⓒ ST 102 063
			Ⓓ ST 100 051
Refreshments	Pub at Broadhembury		
Ordnance Survey maps	Landranger 192 (Exeter & Sidmouth), Explorer 115 (Exmouth & Sidmouth)		

Starting in one of the prettiest villages in South Devon, the route heads uphill along a lane on to a steep, wooded ridge and follows this ridge as it curves left around the head of a combe. On this part of the walk there are outstanding views over a rolling and well-wooded landscape. The descent, along enclosed tracks and field paths, across fields and through woodland, provides some fine views of Broadhembury village and church. Parts of the walk are likely to be muddy after wet weather.

Thatched and colour-washed cottages (many dating from the 17th century) with colourful gardens, an old inn on the village square, a sparkling stream and a medieval church, all combine to make Broadhembury an exceptionally attractive and unspoilt village. The mainly 14th and 15th-century church is distinguished by its tall west tower, a landmark from several points on the walk.

🥾 Start in the square and turn up the lane which passes to the left of the war memorial. Keep along this lane for 1¼ miles (2km), following signs to Dunkerswell and Sheldon, heading uphill. After several steep bends the road continues to climb through woodland and, where it eventually bends right, turn left Ⓐ, at a public bridleway sign, to go on to a path.

The path, which is lined with bluebells in spring, keeps along the right inside edge of sloping conifer woodland. Go through two gates. After the second one, keep ahead to join a track and bear left along it to go through a metal gate. Continue across a sloping field, then bear left to join and follow a wire fence and a line of trees on the left to a metal gate. Go through the gate, continue along an enclosed, hedge and tree-lined path, and, on emerging from the trees, superb views open up to the left over rolling, wooded country.

After going through the next gate, in a line of beech trees, turn right along a fence-lined track and go through another gate onto a lane. Turn left and, after about 200 yds (183m), turn left again Ⓑ along the tree-lined, tarmac drive of the Devon and Somerset Gliding Club. Soon after emerging from the trees, go through a gate beside a cattle-grid and follow the drive to the left. Pass some of the club's hangars and turn right to continue along the left edge of the airfield. Later the tarmac drive becomes a rough track that runs parallel to a wire fence bordering woodland on the left. Keep ahead to eventually reach a bridle-path junction; turn left here **C**, just before a big stand of gorse, to pass through a metal gate. Follow a path downhill

through woodland, soon passing through an old iron gate. Broadhembury church can be seen through gaps in the trees.

Continue along a sunken track and, after a few yards, turn left over a stile, bear slightly right and head across a field to climb a stile into more woodland. After going through a small copse, climb another stile, continue gently downhill along the left edge of a field and turn left over a stile in the bottom corner.

Walk along an enclosed path, climb a stile and continue along what is

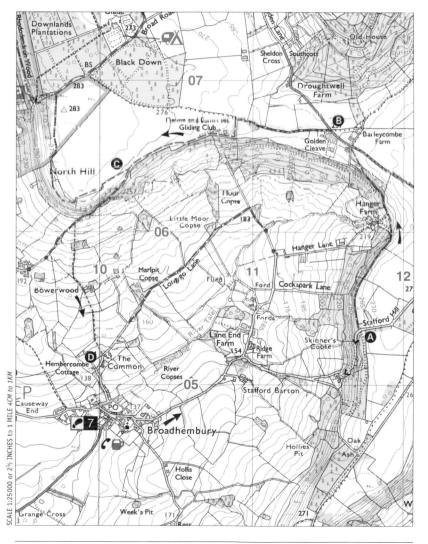

now a wider enclosed track to climb another stile. Keep ahead downhill across the field to another stile. Climb it, keep along the right edge of the next field, by a wire fence and hedge on the right, and where the fence and hedge bend right, keep ahead across the field and climb a stile onto a lane. Turn right  **D** and follow the lane back to Broadhembury. The lane bears right beside the little River Tale; turn left over a bridge to return to the start. ●

Thatched cottages at Broadhembury

Loddiswell and the Avon Valley Woods

		GPS waypoints	
Start	Loddiswell	📷	SX 720 485
Distance	5½ miles (8.75km)	Ⓐ	SX 719 483
Approximate time	3 hours	Ⓑ	SX 721 472
Parking	Loddiswell	Ⓒ	SX 717 470
Refreshments	Pub at Loddiswell, coffee shop at	Ⓓ	SX 719 478
	garden centre over bridge roughly	Ⓔ	SX 730 483
	halfway between Ⓓ and Ⓔ	Ⓕ	SX 731 495
Ordnance Survey maps	Landranger 202 (Torbay & South		
	Dartmoor), Explorer OL20 (South Devon)		

From Loddiswell the route descends across fields into the Avon valley and continues through it, keeping close to the river. The undoubted highlight of the walk is a delightful ramble through the Avon Valley Woodlands that clothe the steep-sided, eastern slopes of the valley, one of the largest areas of woodland in the South Hams. After doubling back to continue through more beautiful woodland on the west bank of the Avon, a steady climb leads back to the start.

Loddiswell is a hilltop village situated high above the western side of the Avon valley. Close to the village centre is the attractive, mainly 14th- to 15th-century church.

📷 The walk starts in the village centre by the Loddiswell Inn. With your back to the pub take the main road ahead through the village. Keep ahead where the road bends left and on the next left bend, by the school, turn right Ⓐ along Towns Lane. The lane leads gently uphill and where it bends right, keep ahead over a stile, at a public footpath sign.

Walk along the left edge of a field, cross a stile and continue along the left edge of the next. Cross another stile. Ahead are attractive views over the gently rolling landscape of the Avon valley. After the third stile head

downhill across the middle of a field, go through a hedge gap by a waymarked stile, and continue down along the right of a field. Look out for a waymark that directs you over a stile by a gate on the right. Continue across the next field, keeping to the right of ponds in the middle, to reach a stone stile. Climb it and turn left on to a sunken, enclosed track – likely to be muddy – to a lane to the right of Hatch Bridge Ⓑ.

Turn left to cross the bridge over the River Avon. Continue along the tree-lined lane and at a public footpath sign just before the second turning on the right, turn left Ⓒ over a stile. Keep ahead across a field, bear left to cross a footbridge over a stream and continue across the field to join and keep beside the riverbank.

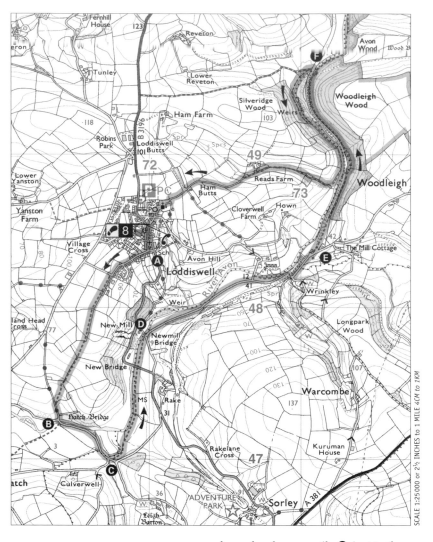

SCALE 1:25 000 or 2½ INCHES to 1 MILE 4CM to 1KM

0	200	400	600	800 METRES	1

KILOMETRES
MILES

0	200	400	600 YARDS	½

Climb a stile, immediately cross a ditch and continue beside the Avon to New Bridge where you turn right up steps to a road. Cross over, turn left down the steps opposite and turn right to continue by the river. Climb a stile in a field corner to reach a lane by Newmill Bridge **D**.

Turn left along the lane for ¾ mile (1.2km), pass under a disused railway bridge after which the lane bears to the left, and, soon after it bears right,

keep ahead over a stile **E** just to the right of the former Loddiswell station. The station was on a branch line that ran from South Brent on the edge of Dartmoor to Kingsbridge before its closure in 1963. Take the path ahead and soon after it enters woodland you reach a stile on the left.

At this point you have a choice of routes. Either keep ahead along the undulating path and, by a waymarked post where you see an old railway bridge over to the left, turn left to join a track and turn right over that

The Avon valley woods

bridge. *Alternatively turn left over the stile and turn right along the disused railway track – this is a permissive route – keeping parallel to the river to reach the bridge.* Either way it is a delightful walk through the Avon Valley Woodlands, owned and managed by the Woodland Trust for public enjoyment and recreation.

After crossing the bridge immediately turn left **F** down steps. After a few yards reach a footpath junction; take the left fork to follow a well-waymarked path back along the other bank of the Avon, climbing a number of stiles. The route proceeds through more beautiful woodland, with one intervening meadow,

crosses several footbridges over side streams and keeps close to the river which flows through what is virtually a thickly wooded gorge.

Eventually the path emerges from the woods to continue across a meadow to a public footpath sign at the far end. Turn right along a path which runs beside a stream on the left, turn left over a footbridge and then turn right to continue along a sunken, enclosed path, now with the stream on the right. Climb a stile and continue gently uphill before going through a metal gate on to a tarmac track. Keep ahead along the steadily ascending lane into Loddiswell, pass to the right of the church then bear left to continue back to the village centre from where you started. ●

Dart Estuary and Dartmouth Castle

		GPS waypoints
Start	National Trust car park at Little Dartmouth. From A379 follow signs right to Dartmouth Castle, then later left, and take the first turning on the right to Redlap and Little Dartmouth	⬛ SX 874 491 🅐 SX 876 486 🅑 SX 884 500 🅒 SX 886 502
Distance	3½ miles (5.5km)	
Approximate time	2 hours	
Parking	Little Dartmouth	
Refreshments	Tearoom at Dartmouth Castle	
Ordnance Survey maps	Landranger 202 (Torbay & South Dartmoor), Explorer OL20 (South Devon)	

Although only a short walk, this is quite an energetic one with plenty of ascents and descents as you follow a rugged stretch of coast around Compass Cove and Blackstone Point, to continue through woodland above the Dart estuary to Dartmouth Castle. Both on the first part of the walk and on the return inland leg, there are superb views along the coast and across the estuary to the castle at Kingswear. Sections of this walk are quite exposed with sheer drops from the cliff, so care should be taken.

🖈 Facing the sea, walk to the right-hand corner of the car park where you go through a kissing-gate to the right of an information board. Take the path ahead along the right edge of fields, by a hedge, go through a gate and descend gently to a kissing-gate. Go through and turn left 🅐 to follow the Coast Path to Dartmouth Castle.

This is a highly attractive walk and easy to follow as you keep along the winding, up-and-down path, looking out for the regular acorn symbols and passing through several gates. The views are superb as the path proceeds around Warren Point and Combe Point, to Compass Cove. Soon after a

right curve at Compass Cove, the path turns right downhill towards the sea, later bearing right at the bottom to a stile. Climb it, turn left and descend steps to a rocky cove. Cross a footbridge over a small inlet and the path bends left around Blackstone Point to continue by the Dart estuary. with striking views of Kingswear Castle on the opposite shore. It later climbs through woodland.

Go through a gate and continue through the beautiful sloping woodland, eventually heading up to a T-junction 🅑 by a fingerpost in front of a house, Compass Cottage. Turn right, in the Dartmouth direction, along a tarmac track and at a

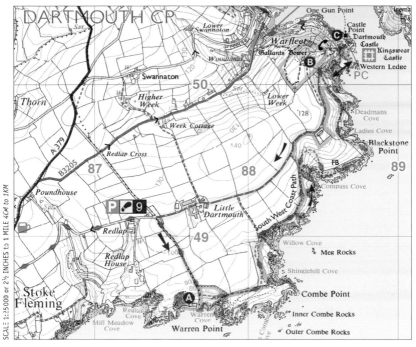

```
0    200    400    600    800 METRES   1
                                        KILOMETRES
                                        MILES
0    200    400    600 YARDS    ½
```

waymarked post a few yards ahead, bear right and head downhill along a path through trees. Look out for another waymarked post which directs you to turn sharp right and follow a zigzag path down a flight of steps. Later the route continues up steps to eventually emerge onto a lane by a parking area. Turn right and descend more steps to Dartmouth Castle **C**, which is about 1 mile (1.6km) south of the town centre. Like its counterpart at Kingswear, it was built in the late 15th century to guard the entrance to Dartmouth harbour and is the earliest artillery fort in the country. As an additional defence, a chain could be hung across the estuary between the two castles. Within the precincts is the mainly 17th-century church of St Petrox, whose tower dominates most views.

From the castle, retrace your route up steps (on the Coast Path) to the lane, turn left and continue up a tarmac track to the fingerpost at Compass Cottage **B**, briefly rejoining the outward route here. Keep ahead, following signs to 'Bridleway, Little Dartmouth'. Continue uphill, along a track which runs through woodland. Go through a gate, continue along the track and where it ends go through a kissing-gate, at a National Trust 'Little Dartmouth' sign. Walk along a path, by a hedge on the right-hand side, which curves left up to a gate, go through and continue along an enclosed track, passing through the farmyard of Little Dartmouth, to return to the start. ●

Kingswear Castle

Gara Rock and Portlemouth Down

		GPS waypoints
Start	Mill Bay, follow signs from East Portlemouth. Alternatively it can be reached by ferry from Salcombe	✒ SX 741 380 Ⓐ SX 752 373 Ⓑ SX 752 370
Distance	3½ miles (5.5km)	
Approximate time	2 hours	
Parking	National Trust car park at Mill Bay	
Refreshments	Hotel at Gara Rock	
Ordnance Survey maps	Landranger 202 (Torbay & South Dartmoor), Explorer OL20 (South Devon)	

From the beach at Mill Bay, a steady uphill climb along a beautiful tree-lined track leads to the coast at the superb viewpoint of Gara Rock. The remainder of the route follows the Coast Path over Portlemouth Down and along the east side of the Salcombe estuary. Towards the end there are particularly fine views across the estuary to Salcombe.

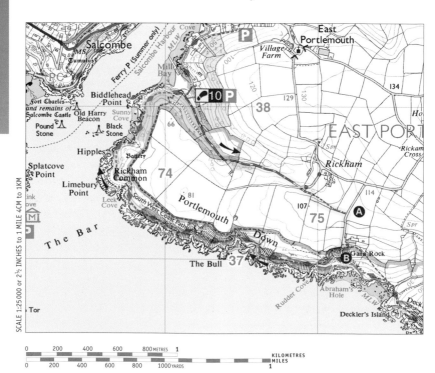

SCALE 1:25 000 or 2½ INCHES to 1 MILE 4CM to 1KM

Looking eastwards from Gara Rock

At the beach turn left, at a public bridleway sign for Rickham, along a track that runs beside the car park. For the next ¾ mile (1.2km) follow this most attractive, shady track, lined by some lovely old trees, steadily climbing uphill to reach a wooden gate. Go through, cross a track, go up some steps and through a gate to continue uphill along an enclosed, sunken track.

Emerge from the trees, pass through a gate, and walk across the field, passing through a hedge gap. On the far side of the next field go through a gate onto a tarmac track **Ⓐ**. Turn right along it towards the coast; where it ends bear right round a low wall,

and turn left. On the right here an unusual thatched lookout provides outstanding views along the coast, especially eastwards to Gammon Head. At the fingerpost turn right **Ⓑ** to join the Coast Path, in the direction of Mill Bay (signposted '2¼ miles' [3.6km]).

Pass below the rock, descend steps and follow the winding and undulating coastal path back to the start. At first the view ahead is dominated by Bolt Head. Later the path curves right to continue along the side of the Salcombe estuary, with fine views across to Salcombe itself on the opposite side. Eventually the path passes above beaches, enters woodland and descends to Mill Bay. ●

The Yealm Estuary

The Yealm Estuary

		GPS waypoints
Start	Noss Mayo	SX 547 474
Distance	4½ miles (7.2km)	**A** SX 541 466
Approximate time	2½ hours	**B** SX 538 464
Parking	Noss Mayo	**C** SX 547 474
Refreshments	Pubs at Noss Mayo	
Ordnance Survey maps	Landrangers 201 (Plymouth & Launceston) and 202 (Torbay & South Dartmoor), Explorer OL20 (South Devon)	

A great advantage of this walk is that the only real climbing, a steady ³⁄₄ mile (1.2km) ascent, comes right at the beginning to reach the coast at The Warren. The rest of the route follows part of Revelstoke Drive, a flat and well-surfaced, 9-mile (14.5-km) track laid out in the 19th century by Lord Revelstoke, a local landowner. The track follows an outstandingly attractive stretch of the coast before bearing right to continue along the beautiful, wooded shores of the Yealm estuary. On this final part of the walk there are superb views across the water to the houses of Newton Ferrers massed on the opposite shore.

Noss Mayo, situated on the south side of Newton Creek, an arm of the Yealm estuary, is the twin village of Newton Ferrers on the north side. Both are extremely attractive and photogenic.

Start by turning left out of the car park, at a public footpath sign to 'The Warren', along an uphill lane. The lane continues as a rough track, ascending steadily all the while, and after ³⁄₄ mile (1.2km) it reaches a lane. Turn left and take the first turning on the right **A** to pass through The Warren National Trust car park.

At the far end pass through a gate and bear right along a hedge-lined track towards the sea. Climb a stone stile and follow the track to the right and you will shortly pick up the Coast Path **B**. Now comes a delightful stretch of coastal walking along the well-constructed Revelstoke Drive, passing through several gates. The views ahead are most impressive looking towards the estuary of the River Yealm and beyond to Plymouth Sound. The track curves right to keep

The Yealm estuary

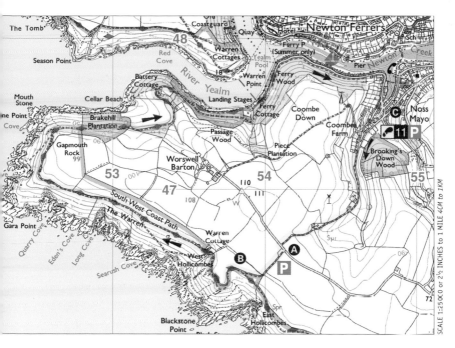

above the Yealm and later continues through attractive woodland fringing the estuary. On this section there are some gates and stiles, and at intervals gaps in the trees reveal fine views over the water.

Looking along the coast from Revelstoke Drive

Continue along a tarmac drive by the estuary and later beside Newton Creek into Noss Mayo. On the opposite side of the creek, the houses of Newton Ferrers, topped by the church tower, make a very attractive scene. Follow the lane to the right, passing in front of cottages. Continue uphill and at a junction turn right **G** along a lane with a 'No Through Road' sign to return to the start. ●

Venn Ottery Common

		GPS waypoints
Start	Tipton St John	SY 090 917
Distance	5 miles (8km)	Ⓐ SY 085 915
Approximate time	2 hours	Ⓑ SY 066 915
Parking	Tipton St John	Ⓒ SY 067 926
Refreshments	Pub at Tipton St John	Ⓓ SY 087 926
Ordnance Survey maps	Landranger 192 (Exeter & Sidmouth), Explorer 115 (Exmouth & Sidmouth)	Ⓔ SY 087 921

From the banks of the River Otter the route climbs steadily and easily, along quiet lanes and enclosed tracks, on to Venn Ottery Common (RSPB reserve). From this elevated expanse of heather and gorse there are tremendous panoramic views over the Otter valley. After descending from the common you continue along more lanes and tracks and there is a short stretch of pleasant riverside walking before returning to the start. This is an undulating walk with no steep or strenuous climbs.

Turn right out of the car park at the bottom end of Tipton St John and cross the bridge over the River Otter. At a T-junction in front of Tipton church, turn left, in the Venn Ottery and Newton Poppleford direction, along a lane which heads uphill and then curves right. Where the lane bends sharply left, keep ahead Ⓐ along a tarmac track with an 'Unmetalled' road sign. After the tarmac track ends, continue along an enclosed track, between hedgebanks, which gradually ascends and then descends to a lane. Keep ahead, steadily uphill, along the lane and just before the top of the hill, turn right Ⓑ, at a public footpath sign, through a hedge gap on to Venn Ottery Common. Follow the path across the open, heather- and gorse-covered common. As you proceed the views are magnificent, especially to the right over the Otter valley.

The path descends to a fork and waymarked post where you take the left-hand path which continues more steeply downhill towards woodland. On entering the trees keep ahead to cross a sleeper bridge. Continue to a footbridge over a stream. Cross this and head uphill along a sunken, enclosed path overhung by trees. Turn left on meeting a tarmac drive and take the first turning on the right to follow a hedge-lined track to a road.

Cross over the road, take the lane ahead, signposted 'Broad Oak and West Hill', and at a crossroads turn right Ⓒ, in the Metcombe and Tipton St John direction, heading downhill. Where the lane bends sharply right, keep ahead, at a public footpath sign 'Unmetalled Road'. Where the tarmac track ends, by a thatched cottage, continue along a hedge-lined track. Follow this attractive, undulating track for 1 mile (1.6km) – there are

SCALE 1:27777 or about 2¼ INCHES to 1 MILE 3.6CM to 1KM

A quiet track below Venn Ottery Common

fine views over the valley ahead –
eventually descending quite steeply,
passing a track (right) and continuing
downhill to reach a road. Turn right
and, at a public footpath sign, turn
left **D** along a tarmac track which
later continues as a rough, hedge-
lined track. Follow the track through
a gate and over a stile onto a disused
railway line. Continue along a faint
path across a field to the banks of the
River Otter.

Turn right alongside the river, pass
into the next field and the river curves
right towards a disused railway bridge.
Go under it and continue by the riverbank to a gate. Go through, bear right
to cross a footbridge over a stream
and continue along a broad, grassy,
partially tree-lined track. Go through
two gates on to a road **E**, turn left
and by the church follow the road to
the left to return to the start.   ●

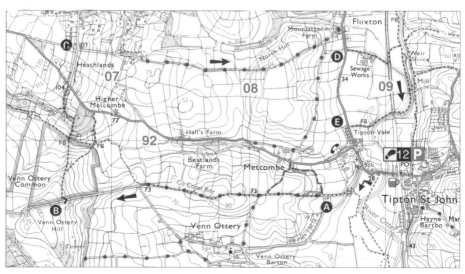

Three Reservoirs Walk

		GPS waypoints
Start	Trenchford Reservoir picnic site at Bullaton Cross	
Distance	6 miles (9.5km)	
Approximate time	3 hours	
Parking	Trenchford Reservoir	
Refreshments	None	
Ordnance Survey maps	Landranger 191 (Okehampton & North Dartmoor), Explorer 110 (Torquay & Dawlish)	

GPS waypoints

- ✐ SX 804 823
- Ⓐ SX 813 826
- Ⓑ SX 824 839
- Ⓒ SX 819 847
- Ⓓ SX 811 843
- Ⓔ SX 807 838
- Ⓕ SX 803 834

The three adjacent reservoirs of Trenchford, Tottiford and Kennick lie in secluded, rolling and well-wooded country on the eastern fringes of Dartmoor. They were constructed between 1860 and 1907 to serve the rapidly growing resorts of Torbay. This pleasant and easy paced walk links them, via quiet lanes, field paths and woodland tracks, passing through attractive conifer woodland and giving some fine views across the water.

✐ Turn left out of the car park and picnic area and turn immediately left again on the lane signposted to Kennick and Tottiford reservoirs. The lane curves left above Trenchford Reservoir and, where it bends left between Trenchford and Tottiford reservoirs, bear right along a tarmac

Quiet countryside on the eastern edge of Dartmoor

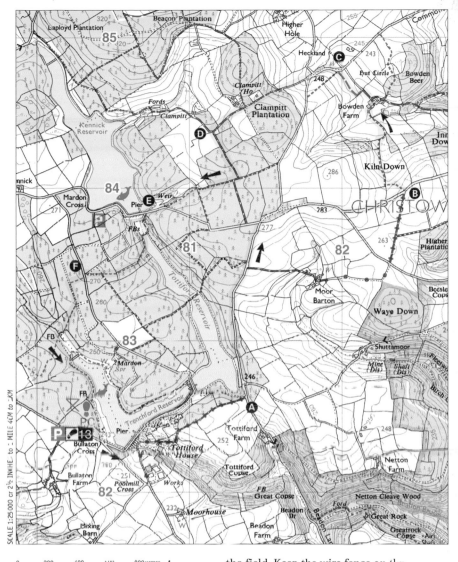

track to a T-junction. Turn left **A** along a narrow, hedge-lined lane for ³/₄ mile (1.2km), heading gently uphill to another T-junction. Turn right. Ignore a left turn to Bridford, and later bear left on an even narrower lane, at an 'Unsuitable for Motors' sign.

At a public footpath sign turn left **B** over a stile and bear left across rough pasture, heading gently downhill to a fingerpost at the field edge. Turn right along the left edge of

the field. Keep the wire fence on the left and follow the path, which eventually leads into trees, with odd yellow spots on tree trunks. This section is likely to be boggy. On reaching the end of the wood follow footpath signs right, and a few yards ahead turn left through a metal gate. Head round the right edge of a field to go through a metal gate on the far side. Continue along the right edge of the next field, following the fence round to the right to go through a metal gate by farm buildings. Turn left along a track, turn left again through the first metal gate and walk slightly uphill along the left edge of a field. By a metal gate and public footpath sign on the left, turn right to head across the field and go through another metal gate on to a lane **C**.

Turn left and, at a meeting of lanes, keep straight ahead, by a 'No Through Road' symbol, along an enclosed, tarmac track, heading uphill. This track becomes rougher, and continues through conifer

conifers. Keep ahead at a fingerpost eventually to climb a stile on to a lane. Turn right to Kennick Reservoir. The view across the water to the right is particularly attractive. On reaching the corner of the reservoir turn left **E** through a gate, at a 'Tottiford Walk' sign, and continue along a path which descends through trees to reach the north end of Tottiford Reservoir, at which point another attractive scene unfolds.

Tottiford Reservoir

Turn right across the end of the reservoir and follow the path to the left to keep alongside it. Look out for where an uphill path leads off to the right (orange arrow) and follow this path through the conifers to climb a stile on to a lane. Turn left and almost immediately turn right, over a stile **F**, at a footpath sign 'Trenchford Reservoir', along a path between bracken and young conifers. Follow the direction of a waymarked post to the left and look out for the next post which directs you to bear right. Continue gently downhill, cross a footbridge over a stream and the path now bends left to reach the side of a footbridge at the end of Trenchford Reservoir.

plantations. Eventually keep ahead downhill, in the Kennick direction, along an attractive, tree-lined track to a T-junction where a plaque marks the Clampitt Quakers Burial Ground (1674–1740). At the time, an age of religious intolerance, the Quakers had to hold their meetings in secluded places like this to avoid persecution.

Turn left **D** along a track, at the next T-junction follow the track to the right and, at a fingerpost a few yards ahead, continue along a gently descending path, still through

At a fingerpost keep ahead, in the 'Trenchford Walk, to Car Park' direction, along a path which bends to the left across a boardwalk and continues along the right edge of the reservoir. Later the path bears right and heads gently uphill through woodland to return to the start. ●

Otter Estuary, East Budleigh and Otterton

		GPS waypoints
Start	Budleigh Salterton. Lime Kiln car park at east end of sea front	🖊 SY 072 820
Distance	6½ miles (10.5km). Shorter version 3 miles (4.75km)	**Ⓐ** SY 075 839 **Ⓑ** SY 069 843
Approximate time	3½ hours. Shorter version 1½ hours	**Ⓒ** SY 068 849 **Ⓓ** SY 967 851
Parking	Lime Kiln car park at Budleigh Salterton	**Ⓔ** SY 073 857 **Ⓕ** SY 078 852
Refreshments	Pubs and cafés at Budleigh Salterton, pubs and café at East Budleigh, pub at Otterton, tearoom at Otterton Mill	
Ordnance Survey maps	Landranger 192 (Exeter & Sidmouth), Explorer 115 (Exmouth & Sidmouth)	

Starting by the Otter estuary, the first part of the route is across riverside meadows. The shorter version returns along the river, but the full walk heads across to the picturesque village of East Budleigh, continues on to Bicton church and rejoins the river at Otterton. The rest of the route is a pleasant and relaxing stroll beside the Otter. This is an easy walk with very little uphill work.

The pleasant little resort of Budleigh Salterton, which first developed during the Victorian era, has a fine beach and all the usual seaside amenities.

🖊 From the entrance to the car park turn right, at a Coast Path acorn post, along a path with a stream on the left. By the playground entrance turn left, and after a few yards turn right, at a public footpath sign 'White Bridge', along a path which is initially hedge-lined but later continues below the wooded embankment of a disused railway on the left. This is an attractive part of the walk with fine views across the meadows on the right.

Keep ahead all the while, negotiating several gates and stiles, and crossing a lane. Keep ahead, and

the path widens into a track, which eventually bends left. At this point keep ahead, by a waymarked post, over a stile and across grass to another stile. Turn right along a track, which curves right towards the river to meet a footpath post **Ⓐ**.

For the shorter version turn right here, through a kissing-gate, and follow the riverside path.

The full walk continues by turning left over a stone aqueduct, raised above the low-lying fields to reduce flooding. Immediately over the aqueduct take the left fork, which leads along the top of a raised embankment above the riverside meadows, curving left to a kissing-gate. Climb this, and continue along

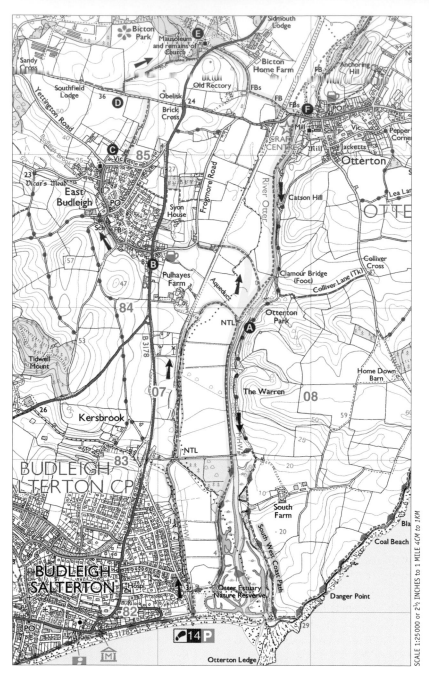

SCALE 1:25000 or 2½ INCHES to 1 MILE 4CM to 1KM

a narrow, tree-lined path, to join a track. Turn right to reach a lane opposite a large farmhouse. Turn left along the lane to meet a road opposite The Rolle Arms **B**. Cross over and keep ahead through East Budleigh. This is a very attractive village with thatched cottages, a stream, and an impressive medieval church that has a pew used by the Raleigh family. Sir Walter Raleigh was born nearby.

The road winds through the village,

passing to the right of the church. At the statue of Sir Walter Raleigh turn right in the Newton Poppleford direction. At a public footpath sign **G** turn left up some steps and go through a kissing-gate. Continue along an enclosed path which passes along the left edge of a playing

The attractive village of East Budleigh

field and curves right to a kissing-gate. Climb this, keep along the right edge of a field, and go through a kissing-gate on to a lane. Turn left and after about 200 yds (183m) look out for a waymarked stile on the right **D**. Climb it, walk along the right edge of a field, descending into a dip, and turn right through a gate – there are blue waymarks – to continue along the left edge of a sloping field, by a line of trees on the left. The field edge curves left to meet a track; keep along it, bearing right to a road.

Just before reaching the road turn left down a walled tarmac drive to see Bicton church. Both the church and the Rolle mausoleum next to it were built in the mid 19th century and there are also the scanty remains of the church's medieval predecessor. Beyond are the gardens of Bicton Park, laid out by the Rolle family. They are open to the public and are well worth a visit. The 18th-century Bicton House is now home to Bicton College. Walk back up the walled tarmac drive and turn left to meet the road. *Turn left along the road, taking great care – this is a fast road and there is no pavement.*

At a public footpath sign opposite Bicton church, bear right **E** along a path, by a wall on the right, that heads down and bears right to continue as a hedge-lined, enclosed

path. Cross a farm drive and keep ahead, later turning left and crossing a footbridge over a stream and then the disused railway line. Continue along the left edge of a field and go through a kissing-gate on to a road. Bear to the left and cross a bridge over a stream. Keep ahead over Otterton Bridge to visit the village of Otterton with its row of thatched cottages, restored mill (open to the public as a working museum, bakery, craft shop, Devon food shop and restaurant) and 19th-century church.

Return to the bridge, cross over and turn left **F** at a public footpath sign to Budleigh Salterton. Go down some steps and continue along a beautiful riverside path. Go through a kissing-gate by a metal bridge and continue beside the River Otter, momentarily joining the outward route to cross the stone aqueduct passed earlier **A**. Bear left through a kissing-gate, joining the shorter walk, for another stretch of attractive riverside walking, passing through several more kissing-gates and crossing a lane en route. Eventually the path bears slightly right away from the estuary, rising above the surrounding marshes and creeks, and, after going through the last gate, continues directly back to the car park. ●

Brixham and Churston Point

		GPS waypoints
Start	Brixham	
Distance	6 miles (9.5km). Shorter version 5½ miles (8.8km)	✐ SX 925 562
		Ⓐ SX 918 568
		Ⓑ SX 901 570
Approximate time	3 hours. 2½ hours for shorter version	Ⓒ SX 898 572
		Ⓓ SX 900 567
Parking	Brixham	Ⓔ SX 905 562
Refreshments	Pubs and cafés at Brixham, beach kiosks (seasonal) at Churston Cove and Broadsands, pub at Churston	
Ordnance Survey maps	Landranger 202 (Torbay & South Dartmoor), Explorer OL20 (South Devon)	

From Brixham harbour the route follows an attractive and well-wooded stretch of coast, via Churston Cove and Elberry Cove, rounding Churston Point to reach the sandy bay of Broadsands. The return leg takes a pleasant inland route, passing Churston Court and church, and regains the Coast Path at Churston Cove for the final ¾ mile (1.2km) back to Brixham. The shorter version returns from Elberry Cove.

For generations of holidaymakers at the nearby resorts of Torbay, a boat trip across the bay to Brixham has always been an essential and highly enjoyable part of the holiday. Despite more recent development as a busy resort, Brixham is still a working port and retains the atmosphere of a traditional fishing village, with narrow streets and rows of colourful houses and cottages rising steeply from the harbour. In 1688 Brixham played a major role in the development of British history when William of Orange landed here to begin his successful campaign to win the throne from his father-in-law, James II. His statue by the harbour is the starting point for the walk.

✐ Face the sea and walk along the left side of the harbour. Where the road bends left uphill, bear right and then left, at a Coast Path sign, and take the winding path at first beside the Outer Harbour and later along the right edge of a large car park. At the

Brixham

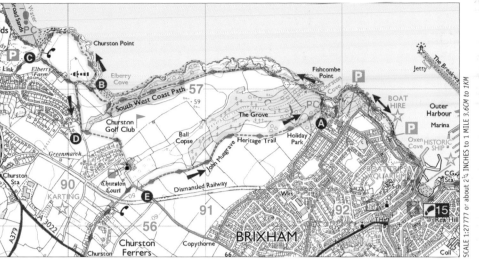

SCALE 1:27 777 or about 2¼ INCHES to 1 MILE 3.6CM to 1KM

far end continue along a tarmac path to a Coast Path sign, climb some steps and at a fork take the right hand lower path that keeps closest to the sea. Ahead are attractive views of Churston Cove.

Where the tarmac path turns sharply left, keep ahead along an enclosed path, then turn right through a wall gap and pass in front of toilets to reach a fingerpost. Turn left, in the direction of Churston Cove. Walk uphill along a tarmac track and at the top turn right to continue along an enclosed path. The path turns left through a metal kissing-gate to a fingerpost and junction of paths **A**. Keep ahead, in the Churston Cove direction, between trees and descend steeply via steps to continue around Churston Cove and across the stony beach. On the other side climb some steps to continue through delightful woodland by Fishcombe Point and later the path bends right, descends more steps and curves downhill to reach Elberry Cove. Walk across the beach and ascend the steps on the far side to reach a path junction **B**.

At this point the shorter version takes the first sharp turning on the left along a path which curves right, continues between hedges and bears left to meet a track coming in from the right. Keep ahead here to rejoin the full walk.

For the full walk keep ahead, pass through a metal barrier and continue along the right edge of an open grassy area around Churston Point. After passing through another metal barrier, a tarmac path curves left alongside the wide, sandy expanses of Broadsands. Keep ahead along the left edge of a car park, to the left of a refreshment kiosk, and turn left **C** along a tarmac track. After passing to the left of Elberry Farm, this becomes a rough track which continues to a T-junction, here rejoining the shorter version.

Turn right along a track, climb a metal stile and continue along a hedge-lined path which heads gently uphill into trees. Take the first turning on the left **D**, go through a metal kissing-gate and continue through trees and later bracken. Follow the path across a golf course, keeping between the lines of yellow posts, and on the far side go through another metal kissing-gate. Bear slightly right along an enclosed, tree-lined path, turn right at a T-junction and after a few yards turn left along a lane to emerge on to another. Continue along the lane which bends right beside Churston church. The medieval church and 17th-century Churston Court standing side by side make an attractive and traditional composition. The church was originally the private chapel of the house which is now an inn.

Follow the lane to the left, at a junction bear slightly left and after a few yards turn left over a stone stile beside a metal gate **E**. Continue along a hedge-lined track. After skirting woodland on the left the track bears right over a stone stile by a metal gate. Walk across a field and on the far side follow the path through woodland and occasional grassy glades. Keep on the main path all the time, eventually descending to a junction of paths by a fingerpost **A**. Turn right through a metal kissing-gate to pick up the outward route and then retrace your steps to the start. ●

Overlooking Brixham harbour

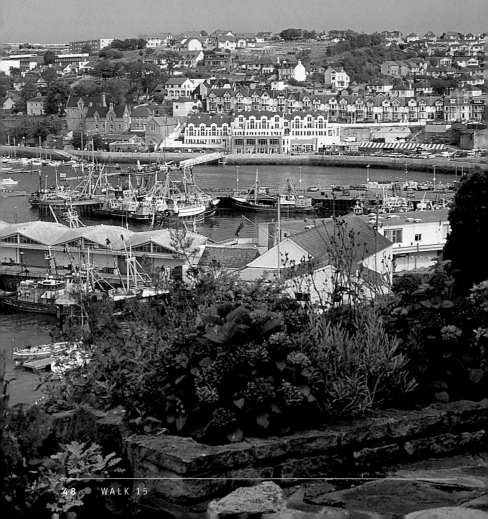

Ashburton and Whiddon Scrubbs

Start	Ashburton	
Distance	5½ miles (8.8km)	
Approximate time	2½ hours	
Parking	Ashburton	
Refreshments	Pubs and cafés at Ashburton	
Ordnance Survey maps	Landranger 202 (Torbay & South Dartmoor), Explorer OL28 (Dartmoor)	

GPS waypoints

- 🖉 SX 755 698
- Ⓐ SX 754 702
- Ⓑ SX 758 709
- Ⓒ SX 753 719
- Ⓓ SX 764 726
- Ⓔ SX 771 719
- Ⓕ SX 765 709
- Ⓖ SX 760 705

After an initial walk across fields by the little River Ashburn, the route climbs steadily through the delightful woodland of Whiddon Scrubbs to Owlacombe Cross. The descent, via a lane and farm tracks, leads back to the edge of Ashburton for the grand finale, the high level Terrace Walk from which there are splendid views over the southern fringes of Dartmoor.

Ashburton is an attractive and unspoilt little town with many old gabled and slate-fronted buildings. In the Middle Ages it was one of the four Stannary Towns (from the Latin *stannum* meaning tin), an administrative centre for the flourishing tin mining industry on Dartmoor at the time. In addition it was an important cloth making town. Its medieval prosperity is reflected in buildings such as the handsome 15th-century church with its imposing tower, and the recently restored St Lawrence's Chapel which in the past has served as a chantry chapel, school and courtroom. Despite its modest size, Ashburton is the largest town within the National Park and makes a good base from which to explore southern Dartmoor.

🖉 Begin in the town centre by walking along North Street, passing the town hall. After ¼ mile (400m)

look out for a public footpath sign to 'Terrace Walk' Ⓐ, turn right up steps and go through an iron kissing-gate at another public footpath sign. Continue, in the Cuddyford Cross direction, along the bottom edge of a sloping field, eventually parallel to the little River Ashburn on the left, to a stile. Climb it, continue by the tree-lined river, climb a stone stile and walk across a field, veering away from the river and field edge, to climb another stone stile and descend steps to a lane Ⓑ.

Cross over, climb steps opposite, at a public footpath sign, go through an iron kissing-gate and bear left along the left edge of a field, by a hedge on the left. Climb a stile, continue along an enclosed, hedge-lined path, climb another stile and cross a stream. The path continues along the bottom inside edge of sloping woodland to a fingerpost. Climb a stile and start on

Beside the River Ashburn in Whiddon Scrubbs

the most attractive part of the walk as you bear left along the bottom edge of Whiddon Scrubbs beside the River Ashburn. Go through a metal kissing-gate, keep ahead and just before reaching a footbridge over the river and lane beyond, turn right, at a public footpath sign to Owlacombe, on to an uphill track **C**.

Initially the track continues through woodland; later it becomes enclosed between hedges and heads steadily uphill to farm buildings. At a T-junction by the farm, turn right on to a tarmac drive which curves left and heads up to emerge on to a lane **D** just south of Owlacombe Cross. Turn right and at a fork continue steeply downhill along the left-hand

lane. At a public footpath sign, half-hidden among bushes, turn right **E** along the tarmac, hedge-lined track to Waye House. In front of the large house turn left, in the direction of Waye Farm. Head downhill and at a fork just before the farm take the left-hand track, and continue steadily downhill.

From now on the noise of traffic on the busy A38 can be heard. After the tarmac track flattens out, by a quarry on the left, it continues as a rough track. Keep ahead and where the track ends in front of a large house, bear to the left, in the direction of the public footpath sign, to a kissing-gate. Go through, bear right to walk in front of the house along the left edge of a long, narrow field, below an embankment on the left, and then follow the field edge to the left, with a school car park right, to go through a kissing-gate. Descend some steps and turn right to reach a lane **F**. Turn right and after a few yards take the first turning on the right (Place Lane), running past the South Dartmoor Community College. Follow the lane around left and right bends to reach a crossroads and then turn left to go through a new suburban housing area built on the edge of Ashburton.

Where a footpath crosses over the road (just before a sign 'Higher Roborough' on the left), turn right **G** along a narrow path, between a hedge and trees on the left and a wall on the right, which continues up between hedgebanks to an iron kissing-gate. Go through and on along the Terrace Walk, a flat, grassy path that follows the contours of the side of the hill giving fine views over the southern edge of Dartmoor and providing a superb end to the walk. After going through a metal kissing-gate the path descends to rejoin the outward route by an iron kissing-gate. From here retrace your steps to the start. ●

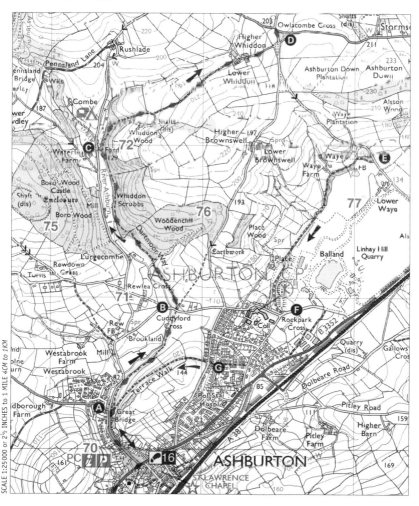

Prawle Point and Woodcombe Point

Prawle Point and Woodcombe Point

		GPS waypoints
Start	National Trust car park at Prawle Point, just over one mile (1.5km) south of East Prawle	✐ SX 774 354
		Ⓐ SX 766 358
Distance	5½ miles (8.75km)	Ⓑ SX 767 361
Approximate time	3 hours	Ⓒ SX 780 363
		Ⓓ SX 786 371
Parking	Prawle Point	Ⓔ SX 794 369
Refreshments	Pubs and café at East Prawle	
Ordnance Survey maps	Landranger 202 (Torbay & South Dartmoor), Explorer OL20 (South Devon)	

Prawle Point is the southern-most tip of Devon and is situated amid some of the most dramatic coastal scenery in southern England. The walk starts by passing the Point and continuing along the coastline almost to Gammon Head. Then follows an inland section, mainly along enclosed paths and tracks, passing through the village of East Prawle and rejoining the coast at Woodcombe Sand. The final part of the route from Woodcombe Point to Prawle Point provides coastal walking at its finest.

✐ Climb a stile in the car park, walk downhill along the right-hand edge of a field to a fingerpost and then turn right over a stile to join the Coast Path. Now comes a spectacular stretch of coastal walking: the path

Gammon Head from Prawle Point

winds around this wild and rugged coastline, passing Prawle Point and continuing around Elender Cove, with the jagged profile of Gammon Head visible in front. There are several gates and stiles, but follow the yellow waymarks and acorn symbols all the time.

At a waymarked post above Maceley Cove turn right Ⓐ, in the direction of the 'Circular Walk'. Head up to the next waymarked post and turn left. Continue steadily uphill, go through a gate, and at a junction of paths and tracks turn right along an enclosed track Ⓑ. Keep along this to a

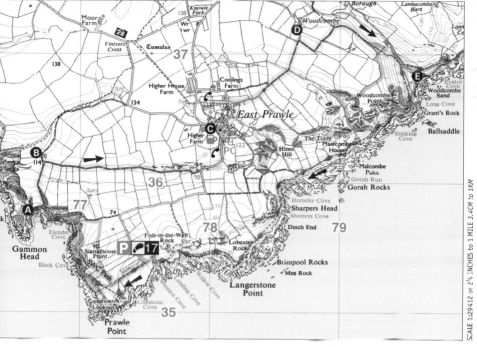

SCALE 1:29412 or 2¼ INCHES to 1 MILE 3.4CM to 1KM

lane. Follow the lane as it heads uphill and curves left into East Prawle.

In the village centre turn right **C** in front of the Pig's Nose Inn and follow a lane to the left. Take the first turning on the right, continue along a curving lane heading uphill, and just in front of a telephone box turn right along a tarmac track. This later becomes a rough track, enclosed between high hedges, and later still narrows to an enclosed path. The path heads down through a wooded area, then heads up and continues along the left edge of a field to a metal gate. Go through and turn right along a track **D**, at a public bridleway sign to Lannacombe Green and Woodcombe Sand. Follow the track around a left bend and where the stony track bends right, keep ahead, at a public footpath/ bridleway sign, along a grassy, enclosed track. At a fingerpost turn right, in the direction of Woodcombe Sand, to continue along a most attractive enclosed path. After going through a gate, the path descends quite steeply through trees along the right side of a combe to a T-junction of paths above Woodcombe Sand.

Turn right **E** to rejoin the Coast Path, initially between bracken and bushes below Woodcombe Point. Start Point can be seen to the left. Keep along the Coast Path back to the start, negotiating several gates and stiles and following the regular acorn symbol waymarks. In particular look out for a sharp left turn, in the Prawle Point direction, along the edge of a field and follow the field edge to the right to continue towards Langerstone Point. Pass below it and soon Prawle Point is seen. Keep along the Coast Path as far as a fingerpost in front of a stile, turn right, in the direction of a public bridleway sign to East Prawle, and retrace your steps to the car park. ●

Start Point and Hallsands

Start	Car park at Start Point. Signposted from the A379 at Stokenham	GPS waypoints
		🖋 SX 820 375
		Ⓐ SX 824 372
Distance	6 miles (9.5km)	Ⓑ SX 829 371
Approximate time	3 hours	Ⓒ SX 802 372
Parking	Start Point	Ⓓ SX 803 383
Refreshments	Café at South Hallsands	Ⓔ SX 817 385
Ordnance Survey maps	Landranger 202 (Torbay & South Dartmoor), Explorer OL20 (South Devon)	

From the prominent headland of Start Point the views along the coast in both directions are outstanding and extensive: northwards across the wide expanse of Start Bay to Berry Head near Brixham, and westwards along one of the most spectacular stretches of the South Devon coast to Prawle Point and beyond to Bolt Head near Salcombe. After a short walk to Start Point, the route continues by heading westwards along the often rocky and dramatic Coast Path to Lannacombe Beach, and then turns inland through a steep-sided, wooded valley. An undulating section along lanes, steep in places, brings you back to the coast at the abandoned fishing village of Hallsands and the final stretch is a steady climb of nearly 1 mile (1.6km) above Start Bay. This is a superb walk but there are narrow paths in places and some fairly energetic climbs.

🖋 Begin by going through a white gate and walking along the tarmac lighthouse road to Start Point. At a fingerpost Ⓐ keep ahead along the road for a short detour to the lighthouse at the tip of Start Point Ⓑ to enjoy the magnificent views that encompass a large stretch of the South Devon coast.

Return to the fingerpost and turn left Ⓐ along the Coast Path which cuts across the narrow neck of the point. The path makes initially for Frenchman's Rock, passing around the jagged pinnacles – *take care here, there are some sheer drops*. On the

next part of the walk the views across Lannacombe Bay to Prawle Point are outstanding as you follow the winding and undulating path along this dramatic and rugged coast to reach Lannacombe Beach.

Go through a gate just before reaching the beach and turn right Ⓒ, leaving the Coast Path, and continue along a narrow, tree- and hedge-lined track – later it becomes a tarmac track – for 1 mile (1.5km) through a thickly wooded and steep-sided valley.

At a T-junction, turn right Ⓓ to continue along a lane which heads uphill to a crossroads at Hollowcombe Head. Keep ahead, in the South Hallsands direction, and the lane soon turns right and descends to the coast above the ruined fishing village of Hallsands (which can be seen from the viewing platform – follow the signs). The village was abandoned after being destroyed during a

violent storm in January 1917 and controversy has raged ever since over why this disaster was actually allowed to happen and was not avoided. One theory blames the sand dredging operations, which had been allowed since 1897, alleging that these had lowered the level of the beach, which used to protect the

Looking across Lannacombe Bay

village. But over the centuries other villages on this stretch of coast have been similarly destroyed by the sea, so perhaps the catastrophe was inevitable.

Turn right **F** on to the Coast Path for a steady, continuous climb of 1 mile (1.6km) to return to the start, enjoying more fine views of Start Point and Start Bay. ●

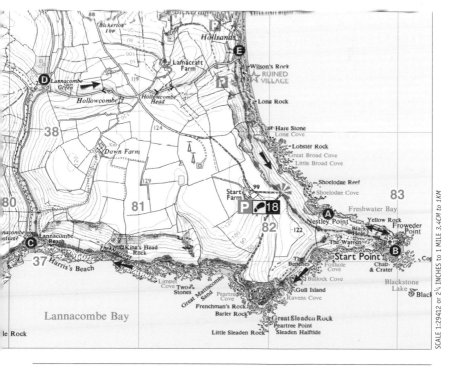

Bolt Head and Salcombe Estuary

Bolt Head and Salcombe Estuary

Start	North Sands car park at south end of Salcombe town	GPS waypoints
Distance	6 miles (9.5km)	🖉 SX 730 382
Approximate time	3½ hours	Ⓐ SX 729 379
Parking	North Sands	Ⓑ SX 713 382
		Ⓒ SX 711 379
Refreshments	Café at North Sands, hotels and café at South Sands	Ⓓ SX 707 377
		Ⓔ SX 705 369
Ordnance Survey maps	Landranger 202 (Torbay & South Dartmoor), Explorer OL20 (South Devon)	Ⓕ SX 722 363
		Ⓖ SX 729 374

Initially this is an undulating inland walk, involving several climbs which bring you to the coast. There then follows a superb stretch of coastal walking to the prominent headland of Bolt Head at the mouth of the Salcombe estuary. The final part of the walk is the most spectacular and energetic, as you proceed around the headland, across the sheer face of Sharp Tor, before descending gently through attractive woodland along the western side of the estuary. On this last stretch there are fine views ahead of Salcombe harbour.

The walk begins by the beach at North Sands at the southern end of the attractive resort, fishing port and sailing centre of Salcombe. Guarding

Looking westwards from Bolt Head

the entrance to the harbour are the sparse remains of a 16th-century artillery fort built by Henry VIII.

🖉 Turn right out of the car park, follow the road uphill, first around a right bend and then a sharp left bend, and at the top, just before the lane drops towards South Sands, turn right Ⓐ along an uphill lane, At a fork continue along the left-hand lane (Moult Road). This shortly becomes a rough track. Keep ahead at a footpath fork and climb steadily to enter an area of woodland, by a public footpath sign. Walk along a narrow path and climb a stile, after which the path descends and continues going as an enclosed,

hedge-lined path. Emerge on to a lane and continue along it, eventually descending past some attractive thatched cottages.

At a fork take the left-hand lane, signed 'Rew and Malborough'. The lane drops then climbs steadily. After ¼ mile (400m) turn left along a tarmac drive **B**, at a public footpath sign to Soar, passing Higher Rew Farm. Keep ahead as signed along a hedge-lined path, by a caravan and camping site on the left. This path curves left and enters a field. Turn right and head uphill along the right edge of a

field to join a track. Continue along this and eventually turn right by a cattle-grid to a meeting of lanes and tracks **C**. Keep straight ahead along the lane to a lane junction in front of a caravan site. Turn left along a lane to Soar Mill Cove, and head downhill to a public footpath sign in front of a thatched cottage **D**.

Turn left to pass in front of the cottage, cross a stream and keep along an enclosed path to pass through a gate. Keep ahead and at a T-junction turn to the right to continue along the enclosed path. Where this path ends, bear slightly left across a field and then head uphill between gorse bushes to a stile at the top edge of the field. Climb it and continue along the right edge of several fields, by a hedge on the right, and over a succession of stiles. After the final stile – by a fingerpost – keep ahead to the clifftop where you reach the coast path **Ⓔ**.

Turn left and follow the path along a rugged and most attractive stretch of the coast following signs for Bolt Head and Salcombe. Keep ahead to pass a Coast Path post and drop to go through a kissing-gate, then follow the Coast Path which climbs on to Bolt Head. On all sides the views along this spectacular and rocky coastline are quite superb.

Follow the clifftop round to the left; climb a stile at a path junction **Ⓕ** then follow the Coast Path right downhill into a hollow with a crag to the right. The path bears left along the edge of the cliff above Starehole Bay and descends into Starehole Bottom, crossing a stream. Go through a gate and continue steadily uphill, via steps, to follow the contours around the sheer face of Sharp Tor. After rounding the tor, descend some steps to continue above the estuary with a succession of attractive views of Salcombe harbour.

Later the path continues through beautiful coastal woods, goes through a kissing-gate and later through another gate, and eventually meets a lane **Ⓖ**. Keep going ahead (downhill), bending first to the left and then sharply to the right to pass the beach at South Sands, and then follow the lane up and down once more to return to the start at North Sands. ●

Bolt Head – the mouth of the Salcombe estuary

Beer and Branscombe

Start	Beer. Cliff Top car park	
Distance	6½ miles (10.5km). Shorter version 4½ miles (7.25km)	
Approximate time	3½ hours. 2½ hours for shorter walk	
Parking	Beer	
Refreshments	Pubs and cafés at Beer, pubs at Branscombe, hotel and tearoom at Branscombe Mouth	
Ordnance Survey maps	Landranger 192 (Exeter & Sidmouth), Explorers 116 (Lyme Regis & Bridport) and 115 (Exmouth & Sidmouth)	

GPS waypoints

- 🖋 SY 228 889
- Ⓐ SY 228 894
- Ⓑ SY 224 892
- Ⓒ SY 211 890
- Ⓓ SY 204 886
- Ⓔ SY 195 884
- Ⓕ SY 196 882
- Ⓖ SY 206 881

This is a highly attractive and varied walk that includes two idyllic villages, a picturesque old church, beautiful woodland, impressive cliffs and coastal views that extend from Lyme Bay to Torbay. From Beer the route heads inland along tracks and field paths to Branscombe. The shorter version proceeds directly to the coast but the full walk continues to Branscombe church and on through lovely coastal woodlands before descending steeply to the beach at Branscombe Mouth. The final stretch of the walk takes the 'Undercliff' route, a narrow and winding path through a landslip below the chalk face of Beer Head, before climbing to the clifftop and continuing back to Beer.

Beer is an exceptionally attractive village, with a sheltered location below the chalk cliffs of Beer Head, stone cottages, a small stream flowing down the main street to the sea and fishing boats drawn up on to the pebble beach. As well as being a fishing village – with incomes occasionally supplemented by smuggling – Beer was, in the past, also renowned for the local freestone, worked since Roman times and used in buildings all over the country. The underground caverns of Beer Quarry Caves are well worth a visit.

🖋 The walk starts at the bottom

end of Cliff Top car park. Take the road (Common Lane) steeply downhill into Beer and turn left up Fore Street to walk through the village, passing to the left of the Victorian church, bearing left along The Causeway Ⓐ. Keep ahead at the next junction, in the Branscombe direction, and turn left along Mare Lane. Head uphill, go round a right-hand bend and where the road bears slightly left towards Beer Head, turn right Ⓑ, still along Mare Lane, and continue up to pass to the right of the Pecorama Pleasure Gardens.

Take the tarmac, hedge-lined track

to the left of the car park entrance. This shortly becomes a rough track – still Mare Lane – which you follow for just under 1 mile (1.6km), passing into fields en route, to a T-junction of tracks **C**. Keep ahead through a kissing-gate, at a public footpath sign. Walk across a field and go through a kissing-gate on the far side. Turn right along the right edge of the next field, and almost immediately left to follow the field edge. Turn right over a stile in the field corner. Take the downhill path through attractive woodland, curving left at a public footpath sign to Branscombe. Continue downhill, ignoring a path right, to a stile. Climb this and continue steeply downhill along an enclosed path – there are fine views from here of Branscombe village and church – to a lane and turn left.

After a few yards the full walk turns right **D** *(at this point the*

*shorter version turns left along the lane to rejoin the full walk at Branscombe Mouth **G**)* along a lane which heads down into the very attractive and rather scattered village of Branscombe. The main part, called Vicarage, is a picturesque collection of cottages grouped around the pub. Another group of cottages lies near the church over 1/2 mile (800m) away. At a T-junction, turn left, in the Sidmouth direction, passing the pub on the right, and continue along the lane, passing a thatched forge (still a traditional working smithy), up to the cruciform church, one of the loveliest village churches in Devon with a fine Norman tower.

Pass through a gate into the churchyard **E** and at a public footpath sign beside the church, turn left down to a stile. Climb this, keep ahead to cross a footbridge over a stream, head steeply uphill along the right edge of a meadow and climb a stile in the corner to enter woodland. Follow a winding path up steps and

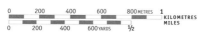

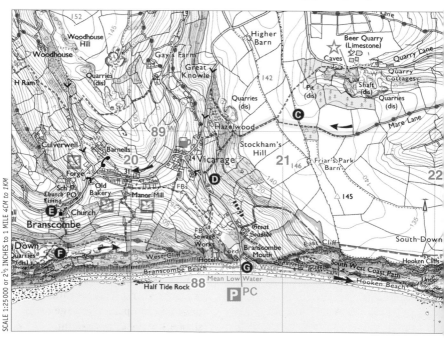

climb a stile. Turn left, still heading uphill through woodland, to reach a T-junction **F**. Turn left along the Coast Path, which you follow for the remainder of the route. The next stage of the walk is particularly attractive as you continue through a beautiful area of woodland, climbing several stiles and with attractive views over Branscombe and the valley to the left.

The Mason's Arms at Branscombe

Eventually you emerge from the trees to descend steeply, via steps in places and always following the acorn sign for the Coast Path, to Branscombe Mouth **G**. It is difficult to believe that the pretty thatched tearoom above the beach was once a coal yard, importing coal from South Wales. Cross a stream, turn right through a kissing-gate and head uphill to a fingerpost. Keep ahead

through a gate, in the 'Coast Path, Beer' direction, and walk along a track through a small caravan site below East Cliff. This is the 'Undercliff' route. Look out for a 'Coast Path' sign which directs you to the right off the track to continue along a narrow, undulating path that twists and turns through the landslip below the cliff. The going is quite difficult in places but eventually the path zigzags up steps to the top of Beer Head, 130m (426ft) high and the most westerly of the chalk headlands on the south coast of England. From here you can enjoy superlative views along the coast almost from Portland Bill on the Dorset coast to Berry Head on the far side of Torbay.

At the top go through a kissing-gate and turn right to follow the Coast Path around Beer Head, negotiating several gates and stiles, and enjoying more superb views as you continue towards Beer. Above Beer beach bear to the left, keeping by a hedge on the left, towards a caravan site and Cliff Top car park. After passing through a kissing-gate, continue along an enclosed path which bends right and eventually passes the car park to emerge on to the road at the starting point. ●

Rippon Tor, Pil Tor and Buckland Beacon

		GPS waypoints	
Start	Cold East Cross, at junction of roads to Newton Abbot, Ponsworthy, Ashburton and Widecombe in the Moor	🖉	SX 740 742
		Ⓐ	SX 746 755
		Ⓑ	SX 741 760
Distance	6½ miles (10.5km). Shorter version 6 miles (9.5km)	Ⓒ	SX 735 759
		Ⓓ	SX 731 757
Approximate time	3½ hours. 3 hours for shorter walk	Ⓔ	SX 728 749
		Ⓕ	SX 727 744
Parking	Cold East Cross	Ⓖ	SX 724 738
Refreshments	None	Ⓗ	SX 720 731
Ordnance Survey maps	Landranger 202 (Torbay & South Dartmoor), Explorer OL28 (Dartmoor)	Ⓙ	SX 735 731
		Ⓚ	SX 736 737

Apart from the initial climb to Rippon Tor, this walk offers dramatic and ever changing views over Dartmoor for relatively little effort. This is very much a 'tor bagging' route that takes in Rippon Tor, Top Tor, Pil Tor, Tunhill Rocks and last, but not least, Buckland Beacon which is a particularly outstanding viewpoint. The full walk includes a ½ mile (800m) diversion to the attractive hamlet of Buckland in the Moor. Without the tors to act as guides, this would be a difficult walk to follow in misty weather and should not be attempted in such conditions unless you are able to navigate using a compass.

🖉 Begin by walking north along the road, in the Haytor and Widecombe in the Moor direction. After ¼ mile (400m) where the wall on the right bends to the right, turn right, and, a few yards ahead, turn right again through the open moor. On joining a wall on the right keep beside it to reach the first group of rocks, the Nut Crackers. Continue uphill, go through a gate and bear left up to Rippon Tor Ⓐ, 1552ft (473m) the first of a series of superb viewpoints on this walk. The views extend over a large area of Dartmoor,

to the Teign estuary and to the coast.

Looking west from the tor, take the obvious path towards the bottom right-hand corner of the down below, just before a road junction. Pass through a small gate in the wall at the bottom, then bear left through a gate by the cattle-grid to reach Hemsworthy Gate Ⓑ. Cross the Ashburton road, keep ahead across a small parking area and follow a path that heads up to Top Tor. From here, turn left and make your way across to the more impressive Pil Tor Ⓒ. Bear right to pass through the middle of

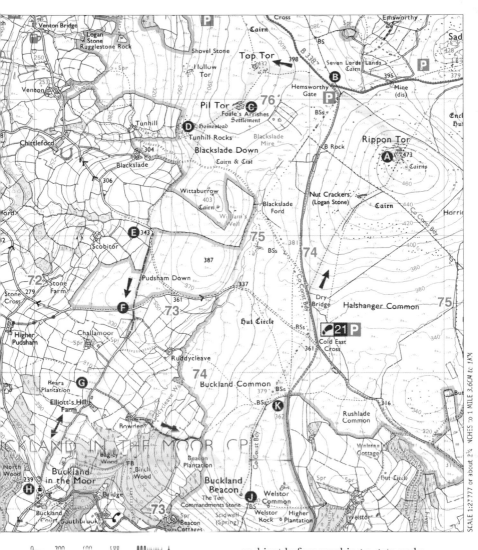

SCALE 1:27,777 or about 2¼ INCHES to 1 MILE 3.6CM to 1KM

the rocks and follow a track gently downhill to the next group, Tunhill Rocks. All the way the views are glorious, especially over the Webburn valley to the right where Widecombe in the Moor church tower is a prominent landmark.

At Tunhill Rocks turn left **D**, head downhill to a wall corner and continue alongside a wall on the right to a ladder-stile. Climb this, continue along the right edge of moorland, still by a wall on the right,

and just before reaching a gate and a corner, bear left to climb another ladder-stile and turn right down to a lane. Turn left, immediately follow the lane around a right-hand bend and, where it bears slightly left, keep straight ahead **E** along a path across Pudsham Down, by a hedgebank on the right. After the hedgebank turns right, keep ahead, between gorse, bracken and heather, to a road **F**. Cross over, go through a gate, at a public bridleway sign, and continue downhill along the attractive, hedge- and partially tree-lined track ahead – it later becomes a tarmac track.

After nearly ¹/₂ mile (800m) another tarmac track leads off to the left G. *Turn left along it if you wish to omit the detour to Buckland in the Moor, otherwise keep ahead, descending more steeply, to emerge on to a road opposite the church* H. The detour is worth the extra effort for Buckland is a most appealing hamlet of thatched, granite cottages that extend eastwards from the medieval church along the lane below the steep, wooded slopes of Buckland Beacon.

Retrace your steps to G and turn right along the tarmac track. The track descends to Bowden Farm. Opposite the farm entrance bear left through a metal gate on a public bridle-path. The rough track crosses a stream, ascends along the left edge of a plantation and continues between walls to pass through a gate onto moorland. Keep ahead for a few yards, then turn right; then take the right fork, soon bearing left to pick your way uphill to gain Buckland Beacon J. At 1250ft (381m), this is another magnificent viewpoint looking over the thickly wooded and steep-sided Holne Chase and Dart gorge, with open moorland on the horizon and Buckland in the Moor church immediately below. Two granite stones here were carved with the Ten Commandments in 1928 by the same man who arranged for 'My Dear Mother' to be inscribed on the clock face of Buckland church instead of the usual numerals.

With your back to the view, take the path which keeps alongside a wall on the right. Where the wall curves right K keep ahead uphill on a grassy path. Descend to meet a lane and turn right along it to return to the start at Cold East Cross. ●

Towards Widecombe church from Tunhill Rocks

Torcross, Slapton Ley and Stokenham

		GPS waypoints
Start	Torcross. Car park on north side of village	🥾 SX 823 424
Distance	7 miles (11.25km)	Ⓐ SX 817 443
Approximate time	3½ hours	Ⓑ SX 821 443
		Ⓒ SX 813 445
Parking	Torcross	Ⓓ SX 802 434
Refreshments	Pubs and cafés at Torcross, pubs at Stokenham	Ⓔ SX 806 432
		Ⓕ SX 807 427
Ordnance Survey maps	Landranger 202 (Torbay & South Dartmoor), Explorer OL20 (South Devon)	Ⓖ SX 810 420
		Ⓗ SX 820 413

There is a great variety of terrain and considerable historic interest on this walk. The scenic variety includes a walk beside the raised shingle beach of Slapton Sands, the lagoon and marshlands of Slapton Ley Nature Reserve, some pleasant woodland and a stretch along the Coast Path. On the final descent into Torcross a superb view unfolds along the length of Start Bay, with the whole of the route spread out before you. Historic interest ranges from the medieval church at Stokenham to a hitherto largely unknown Second World War disaster, commemorated by the tank at the start of the walk. The first 2½ miles (4km) are fairly flat; after that be prepared for several lengthy and fairly steep climbs.

The black Sherman tank at the south end of the car park was recovered from the seabed in 1984 and placed here as a memorial to over 900 US servicemen, killed by a surprise German attack in April 1944 while rehearsing for the D-Day landings. News of the tragedy was suppressed at the time and for many years it remained largely unknown until a local man, Ken Small, wrote a book about it and played a major role in organising the tank memorial.

🥾 At the north end of the car park a path leads off through a gate and runs parallel to, and just below, the road across the narrow causeway between the sea and the freshwater lagoon of Slapton Ley. After 1¼ miles (2km) the path reaches a lane. Turn left along this and after crossing Slapton Bridge turn left Ⓐ through a gate, at a public footpath sign, to follow a path through Slapton Ley Nature Reserve, an important habitat for wildfowl. The path, attractively tree-lined in places, keeps by the water and proceeds up and down steps, over stiles and across boardwalks. After bearing right along the right edge of a marshy area, you reach a fingerpost in front of a stile. Do not climb the stile but turn left **B**, in the 'Permissive Route, Slapton Village' direction. Continue across more boardwalks, bending left along the left edge of the marsh to another fingerpost. Keep ahead, in 'Deer Bridge' direction, along a tree-lined path to emerge on to a lane **C**.

Turn left over Deer Bridge and follow the lane steadily uphill for 1 mile (1.5km), curving gradually left to reach a junction of lanes at Coleridge Cross. At a public footpath sign to Stokenham **D** bear to the left, then head diagonally right across a field, aiming for a tall footpath post. Go through a gate and continue straight across the next field to go through a hedge gap on to a lane **E**. Turn right downhill into Stokenham, an attractive village of whitewashed cottages, some of which are thatched, and presided over by an unusually large and imposing 15th-century church – a fine example of the Perpendicular style. Like other

Stokenham

villages in the area, Stokenham was evacuated in 1943 so that American troops could use it while making preparations for D-Day.

At a T-junction, turn right and almost immediately turn sharp left down a narrow, enclosed lane to another T-junction. Turn left, follow the lane as it bends right to pass in front of the church, and continue down to the main road **F**. Cross over, take the narrow, uphill lane opposite to a T-junction **G**, keep ahead through a metal kissing-gate, at a public footpath sign to Beeson, and continue uphill across a field towards a lone sycamore. Near the top keep by a wire fence on the right to go through another metal kissing-gate and continue to a tarmac track. Turn left along this through woodland. Later the track bears left and continues as a rough track down to a thatched cottage. Walk along a path to the left of the cottage and continue gently downhill along the left inside edge of woodland to a stile. Climb this, cross a track, climb another stile opposite and bear to the left to keep alongside the right edge of a sloping field.

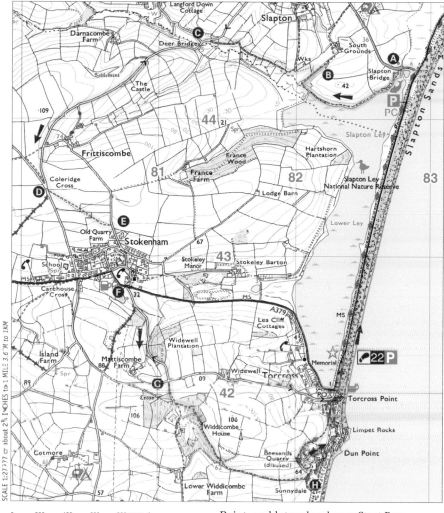

SCALE 1:27777 or about 2¼ INCHES to 1 MILE 3.6 ″M to 1KM

0	200	400	600	800 METRES	1
					KILOMETRES
					MILES
0	200	400	600 YARDS	½	

About 50 yds (46m) before reaching the field corner, climb a stile on the right and continue down an enclosed path to reach a T-junction ⓗ. Turn left to join the Coast Path, heading uphill through woodland, and follow this as it curves right, around the rim of Beesands Quarry, before descending to a gate. Go through the gate to emerge from the trees and continue downhill along a grassy path to another gate. From this path the view left to Beesands and Start

Point, and later ahead over Start Bay, Slapton Sands and Slapton Ley is magnificent, and almost the whole route of the walk can be seen.

Go through the gate and continue downhill along an enclosed path which eventually bends sharp right down to a tarmac track. Follow the track round a left bend and, at a waymarked post, turn sharp right. Walk along a rough track, passing in front of houses, until this narrows to a path and descends steps to the promenade at Torcross. Continue along here and turn left to cross the main road and reach the car park. ●

Widgery Cross and Great Links Tor

		GPS waypoints
Start	Car park ¼ mile (400m) along lane that leads north-eastwards from the A386 by the Dartmoor Inn	 SX 525 854
		Ⓐ SX 530 857
Distance	6½ miles (10.5km)	Ⓑ SX 539 855
Approximate time	3½ hours	Ⓒ SX 551 861
		Ⓓ SX 550 867
Parking	Car park to north east of Dartmoor Inn	Ⓔ SX 552 871
		Ⓕ SX 545 887
Refreshments	Dartmoor Inn near start	Ⓖ SX 530 863
Ordnance Survey maps	Landrangers 191 (Okehampton & North Dartmoor) and 201 (Plymouth & Launceston), Explorer OL28 (Dartmoor)	

Two tors are climbed on this walk: the first ascent, to Widgery Cross on the summit of Brat Tor 452m(1480ft), is steep; the second, to the impressive bulk of Great Links Tor 586m (1925ft), is relatively easy. After descending from Great Links Tor, the route is along clear and well-defined tracks, mostly using disused railway lines that used to serve a peat works. The entire walk is across open moorland on the western edge of Dartmoor and the views are both tremendous and extensive, especially westwards towards Cornwall and Bodmin Moor. But there is some rough walking and you are advised not to attempt this in bad weather or misty conditions unless you are an experienced walker able to navigate using a compass.

Widgery Cross, Brat Tor

Start by walking along the grassy track that leads out of the top left corner of the car park and runs roughly parallel to the vehicle track on the left. Immediately there is a fine view of both the tors that are to be climbed: Brat Tor, which is crowned by Widgery Cross, slightly to the right and Great Links Tor ahead. Continue along the track which descends fairly gently before joining the vehicle track Ⓐ near a ford, footbridge and stepping stones across the River Lyd. This is a

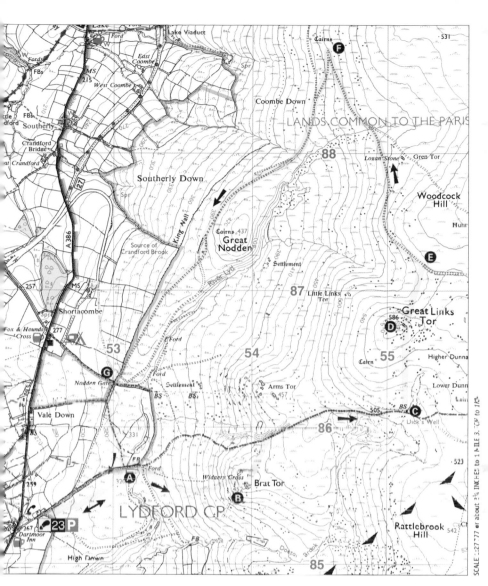

| 0 | 200 | 400 | 600 | 800 METRES | 1 |
| 0 | 200 | 400 | 600 YARDS | | 1/2 |

KILOMETRES
MILES

delightful spot.

Cross the river and bear half-right off the track to continue along a clear, grassy path heading steeply up to the summit of Brat Tor **B**. This is quite a strenuous climb but the view from the top, over Dartmoor and West Devon, is superb. Immediately below are Lydford Castle and church. Widgery Cross was erected in 1887 to commemorate Queen Victoria's

Golden Jubilee.

At the summit face due east and bear half-left to head across grassy moorland in the direction of the prominent bulk of Great Links Tor on the skyline. On meeting a sunken track, turn right and follow this rocky, grassy old tin miners' track until you reach a boundary stone on the left, roughly where the embankments lining the track peter out. At the stone, turn left **C** and continue gently uphill across the rough, open moor to the

The view west from Great Nodden

triangulation pillar on Great Links Tor **D**, a most impressive collection of rocks and another magnificent viewpoint over the area.

Keep on in roughly the same direction, descending across rough and uneven terrain towards the clear track ahead. This is a disused railway track built in 1879 to transport peat from the Rattlebrook Peat Works beyond Great Links Tor. It closed down in 1955. Turn left **E** along the track and follow it, as it curves first to the right and later slightly to the left, as far as a junction of tracks **F**. All the way the views to the left across West Devon are superb.

At the junction turn sharp left, almost doubling back, along a track that has been in view below on the left for some time. This clear and well-surfaced track, still part of the old peat line, curves right over the lower slopes of the smooth, rounded hill of Great Nodden, giving more fine views, and descends gently. At a fork take the right-hand track which continues to descend to meet a wall on the right. Where the track curves left, just before reaching the wall corner on the edge of the moor, keep ahead to the corner, Nodden Gate **G**. Turn right through a gate, turn left, and left again through another gate. Turn right, at a public footpath sign, to continue along the right edge of the moor, by a wall on the right. At a fingerpost turn half-left, head gently uphill across grass and over the brow. Descend equally gently, passing a football post, making for a metal gate and public footpath sign. Climb a stone stile to the right of the gate and turn half-right **A** along a grassy track – not fully right on to the vehicle track – to return to the start.●

Yes Tor and High Willhays

Start	Okehampton Moor Gate. From Okehampton follow signs to Okehampton Camp and Moor Gate is just beyond the camp	**GPS waypoints**	
		🖉	SX 591 931
		Ⓐ	SX 587 924
Distance	6 miles (9.5km)	Ⓑ	SX 582 919
		Ⓒ	SX 585 908
Approximate time	3½ hours	Ⓓ	SX 580 901
		Ⓔ	SX 580 899
Parking	Park on grass on edge of open moor just past Moor Gate	Ⓕ	SX 580 891
Refreshments	None		
Ordnance Survey maps	Landranger 191 (Okehampton & North Dartmoor), Explorer OL28 (Dartmoor)		

Considering that this walk is to the highest points on Dartmoor – and indeed the highest in England south of the Pennines – this is a relatively easy route, mostly on clear tracks and with steady, rather than steep climbs. The only rough moorland walking is the final part of the ascent to Yes Tor 619m (2030ft), from where it is an undulating stroll to High Willhays 621m (2039ft). The descent could hardly be more straightforward. Still, this is not a route to be tackled in bad weather unless you are an experienced walker able to navigate with a compass. *On good days it is most exhilarating, with glorious views over northern Dartmoor and across mid Devon to the edge of Exmoor.* Part of the walk enters the Okehampton Military Range, which is used for live firing on a limited number of days. The boundaries are marked by red and white posts and by red and white warning noticeboards. Details of firing times can be obtained from National Park information centres or www.dartmoor-ranges.co.uk Do not enter the range at firing times when the red flags are flying, and do not pick up any metal objects while walking within the Range area.

🖉 Walk down the lane towards Moor Gate. Cross the river, then turn left (before Moor Gate) along a tarmac track, above Moor Brook on the left and by a wall bordering the army camp on the right. From the start there is a grand view ahead of West Mill Tor and Yes Tor. Stay on the tarmac track to pass Anthony Stile – a stile and public footpath sign in the wall across grass to the right – and carry on to a junction where the tarmac track turns left Ⓐ. Keep ahead along a rough track that climbs gently over Black Down and at a junction of several tracks, bear left **B** on to a track that you can see heading across grassy moorland and then climbing up to the col between West Mill Tor and Yes Tor.

Follow this track as it winds steadily up and at the col where the track peters out, turn right **C** across rough and boggy grassland towards a path that can be seen leading up to the summit of Yes Tor. Cross a stream (on granite boulders) and continue

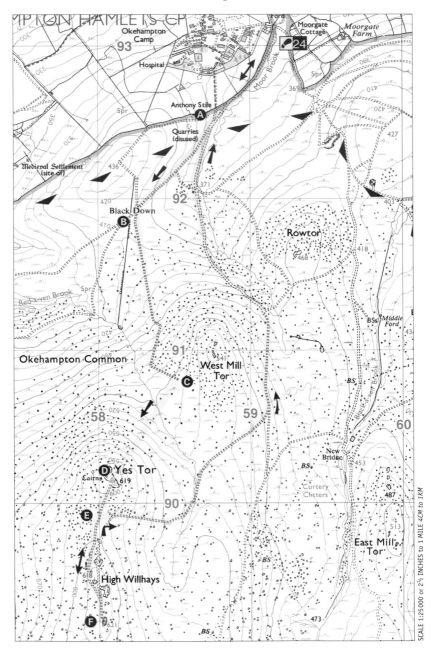

steeply up to the triangulation pillar **D**. This is the second highest point on Dartmoor and not surprisingly is a magnificent vantage point with views to the south and east over a large area of Dartmoor, westwards in the direction of Bodmin Moor, and northwards across mid Devon to the distant outline of Exmoor.

High Willhays is straight ahead. Follow a clear and well worn track across a broad ridge; the col **E** is so shallow that it is almost a flat walk. Although it is the highest point on

The path to High Willhays from Yes Tor

Dartmoor, High Willhays is less impressive than Yes Tor but the views from it are equally outstanding and the summit **F** has a distinct feeling of remoteness.

Retrace your steps to the col just below Yes Tor **E** and turn right along a broad, stony track which descends steadily and fairly gently, curving left. Ford a stream and continue down, at first below Yes Tor and later below West Mill Tor, enjoying more fine views. Keep straight ahead on the main track all the time – later it is tarmac – and follow it back to the start.

Sidmouth, Salcombe Regis and Weston Combe

		GPS waypoints
Start	Sidmouth	SY 125 871
Distance	8 miles (12.8km)	Ⓐ SY 128 878
Approximate time	4 hours	Ⓑ SY 129 884
Parking	Sidmouth	Ⓒ SY 132 886
Refreshments	Pubs and cafés at Sidmouth	Ⓓ SY 143 885
Ordnance Survey maps	Landranger 192 (Exeter & Sidmouth), Explorer 115 (Exmouth & Sidmouth)	Ⓔ SY 151 888
		Ⓕ SY 160 892
		Ⓖ SY 163 880

The first part of the walk, a gentle stroll through a park beside the little River Sid, is the easiest. This is followed by a long, steady climb over Salcombe Hill to the attractive village of Salcombe Regis. Field paths lead on to the Donkey Sanctuary near the head of Weston Combe and then there is a gentle descent through the beautiful, well-wooded combe to the coast at Weston Mouth. The walk along the Coast Path back to Sidmouth is a strenuous, switchback route of nearly 3 miles (4.8km) over a series of steep and daunting-looking cliffs. Take your time and have frequent rests in order to enjoy the magnificent coastal views on this section of the walk, especially the view over Sidmouth on the final descent of Salcombe Hill Cliff.

The genteel resort of Sidmouth occupies a sheltered position between steep red sandstone cliffs. It became fashionable during, and just after, the Napoleonic Wars when the English aristocracy were cut off from their usual continental haunts, and the town possesses a number of dignified Georgian and Regency villas, many of them now hotels. Royal prestige was bestowed on the town when the future Queen Victoria stayed here as a young girl with her parents in 1819.

The walk starts on the promenade, built in 1837, at the end of Station Road in front of the Bedford Hotel. Facing the beach turn left along the promenade, turn left again by the Royal York & Faulkner Hotel and walk through the town centre. Opposite the Radway Cinema turn right along Salcombe Road and just after crossing the bridge over the River Sid, turn left Ⓐ along a tarmac path that continues through an attractive park beside the river for nearly ¾ mile (1.2km).

At a T-junction, turn right Ⓑ along a lane up to a road, turn left and where the road bears slightly right, bear right Ⓒ up hedged Milltown Lane. Where the lane ends continue uphill, at a 'public bridleway' sign, along an enclosed, tree-lined path. At

Looking towards Sidmouth from the coast path

a fork take the left-hand path and climb a flight of steps to a T-junction of paths and tracks. Turn left along a track heading steadily uphill through attractive woodland. The track bears right to emerge from the trees; keep ahead to eventually go through a gate and onto a road **D**. Turn left, and at a fork by a war memorial, take the right-hand road and continue steeply downhill into Salcombe Regis, a quiet and secluded village of thatched cottages which has an attractive medieval church.

Just past the church turn right along a lane which heads uphill between trees. About 100 yds (92m) after emerging from the trees climb a stile on the left **E** with a public footpath disc. Walk along the left edge of a field, follow the field edge round to the right, climb a stile and keep ahead across a field to climb

another. Continue along the left edge of the next field, climb the stile slightly to the left in the field corner (not the one in the hedge in front) and continue through a kissing-gate. With a wooden fence left keep ahead to pass through another kissing-gate. Keep ahead to pass through two more. Continue, with a hedge left, to pass through a metal gate on to a lane. Turn left and almost immediately right through a gate, following the pedestrian route through the Donkey Sanctuary. This is a home for unwanted and neglected donkeys who are looked after for the rest of their lives and it is open to the public.

At a public footpath sign to Weston Mouth, bear right **F**, and walk downhill on a narrow path between wooden fences, climbing two stiles at the bottom. Turn right, at another public footpath sign to Weston Mouth, along a path that continues gently downhill through the beautiful, wooded Weston Combe, negotiating two stiles on route. On meeting a track, bear left and continue down through the combe, eventually reaching a kissing-gate and a 'Coast Path' sign in the bottom left-hand corner of a meadow. Turn right **G** in the Salcombe Mouth direction, onto the Coast Path.

This is the start of the climb up Lower Dunscombe Cliff. Walk steeply uphill along the left edge of the meadow, go through a kissing-gate and continue steeply up through trees and along a winding path. Turn sharp left, following the regular Coast Path acorn symbols, to emerge on to the open, grassy clifftop. The view to the east of Weston Cliff is particularly impressive. The path curves inland to a fingerpost, bears left down steps, heads up and bears left again to pass around the deep ravine of Lincombe, later rejoining the top of the cliffs and continuing along to Higher Dunscombe Cliff. Now come superb views looking westwards along the coast to Sidmouth with Torbay on the horizon.

After passing a National Trust sign to Combe Farm comes the steep descent to Salcombe Mouth, via steps in places. Opposite is the daunting sight of Salcombe Hill Cliff. Turn right along the bottom edge of a meadow, above the wooded combe, at a finger-post turn left, in the Sidmouth direction, to cross a footbridge over a stream, and then turn left on the other side to keep above Salcombe Mouth.

Now follows one of the most energetic parts of the walk, the steep climb up Salcombe Hill Cliff. Continue along the clifftop, go through a gate and just beyond it is a viewfinder at the start of the descent into Sidmouth. Turn half-right – not

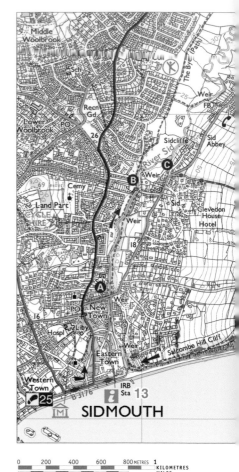

fully right – in the 'Coast Path, Sidmouth Seafront' direction, along a narrow path through grass from which there is a glorious view of the whole of Sidmouth spread out before you.

At a path junction by a bench bear left on the Coast Path and descend steeply via steps through woodland, keeping a constant look out for the acorn symbols. A brief emergence into open country is followed by more woodland, then comes an enclosed section and finally the path keeps to the left edge of a meadow, descending all the while. At this point the Coast Path has been diverted

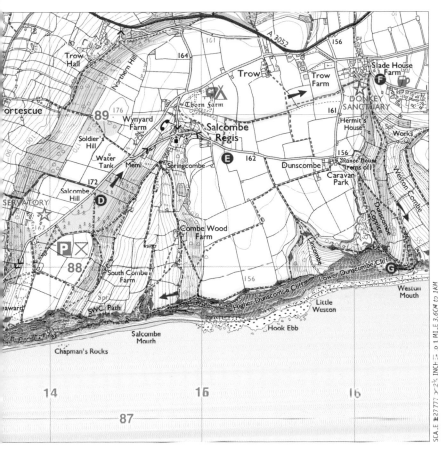

SCALE 1:27,777 or 2¼ INCH = 0 1 MILE 3.6CM to 1KM

because of unstable cliffs ahead. Turn right on to a tarmac path along the top edge of a meadow, by a hedge on the right, later continuing along an enclosed, tarmac track. At the end of this track turn left down Laskeys Lane between houses. Where the lane bends right, bear left along another tarmac track, and where this ends turn right downhill along a road (Cliff Road). Where the road bends right, keep ahead along a tarmac path which curves left to rejoin the original line of the Coast Path. Turn right, descend a flight of

steps and at the bottom cross a bridge over the River Sid. Keep ahead on the promenade to return to the start. ●

The start of the descent into Sidmouth

Princetown, Dartmoor Railway and Leather Tor

Start	Princetown	**GPS waypoints**	
Distance	10 miles (16km)	SX 589 735	
Approximate time	5 hours	Ⓐ SX 565 732	
Parking	Princetown, by the High Moorland Visitor Centre	Ⓑ SX 562 728	
		Ⓒ SX 555 715	
		Ⓓ SX 560 708	
Refreshments	Pubs and cafés at Princetown	Ⓔ SX 559 703	
Ordnance Survey maps	Landrangers 191 (Okehampton & North Dartmoor) and 202 (Torbay & South Dartmoor), Explorer OL28 (Dartmoor)	Ⓕ SX 561 695	
		Ⓖ SX 574 700	
		Ⓗ SX 601 708	

Although this is a long walk amid some of the wildest and emptiest terrain on Dartmoor, most of it is on clear tracks with no rough or strenuous sections, apart from the climb to Sharpitor and Leather Tor, and the subsequent descent to Burrator Reservoir. The area around the reservoir provides some pleasant woodland walking; otherwise the route is entirely across open moorland with extensive and panoramic views, especially from the two tors that are climbed. This walk is, however, in inhospitable country and should not be attempted in bad weather unless you are experienced in such conditions and are able to navigate using a compass. *Save the walk for a fine day when you will be able to savour the high moorland to the full.*

'Grim' and 'bleak' are adjectives which are often used to describe Princetown, especially if seen on a grey and misty day. This is partly as a result of its location and surroundings, high up on the open moor, and partly because it is home to Dartmoor's best known, if least attractive, building – the prison – which appears to match its setting perfectly. Princetown was founded by Sir Thomas Tyrwhitt in the early 19th century and was named after the Prince Regent (later George IV), from whom the land was leased. Tyrwhitt hoped to develop the area into a flourishing agricultural community and to attract people here. It was also he who suggested the building of the prison to house French prisoners from the Napoleonic Wars. The prison was built in 1806, closed down at the end of the wars in 1815 and reopened for convicts in 1850. In recent years Princetown has developed into something of a tourist centre with the creation of the High Moorland Visitor Centre which is well worth a visit.

From the car park entrance turn left. Pass the fire station and then bear left on the track signposted 'Disused Railway'. Go through a gate and continue along the track, skirting the edge of a small conifer wood and heading out across open moorland. The railway, which was originally known as the Plymouth and Dartmoor Railway, was built by Sir Thomas Tyrwhitt as a horse-drawn tramway as part of his plan to develop the area around Princetown. It was later converted to a steam-driven railway and mainly transported granite from the local quarries. It was closed down in 1956 and now provides a superb, flat walking and cycling route traversing some of the wildest parts of Dartmoor, with grand views over the countryside in all directions.

Approaching Leather Tor from Sharpitor

Follow the winding track for 1¼ miles (3km), eventually curving right to an intersection of tracks **A**. Turn left along a track that heads gently downhill to join a wall on the left and follow this wall, to the left, to reach a T-junction of tracks **B**. Turn left here, rejoining the disused railway track, and follow it as it curves first to the right, giving fine views ahead over the Walkham valley, and then to the left around the base of Ingra Tor. Where the track starts to curve right again, turn left off it **C** on to a track that heads uphill. This track later peters out but continue in the same direction to emerge on to a road by a small car park **D**. Cross over and head uphill across rough, trackless moorland, making for the prominent rocky pile of Sharpitor ahead **E**, another magnificent viewpoint.

From here bear to the left and make your way across to Leather Tor,

another superb vantage point, especially looking southwards across Burrator Reservoir. Unless you want to climb to the top, walk past the tor, keeping it about 100 yds (92m) to your left. Before reaching two outlying rock stacks bear right downhill across rough ground towards the trees and reservoir below. Turn left on reaching a wire fence and wall, and pick your way downhill between rocks, bracken and gorse. Keep the wall on your right to reach a lane by a water channel and a restored cross. Turn left **F** along a track that keeps between the bottom edge of the moor, on the left, and woodland on the right. Bear right to cross a channel. This is the Devonport Leat, which is 15 miles (24km) long and was built in the 1790s to bring water from Dartmoor to the naval base at Devonport.

Continue through conifer plantations, keeping on the main track all the while, descending gently and curving right to cross Leather Tor Bridge over the infant River Meavy. Turn left and at a fork a few yards ahead, take the right-hand track which curves right and heads gently uphill, eventually bearing right to a T-junction. Turn left **G** to continue along the right edge of the conifers, between hedge-banks faced with granite blocks. At the corner of the plantation pass between gateposts and continue once more across wild and lonely moorland. Two more crosses can be seen from the track: the first on the skyline above, the second further on, to the right. Eventually the track curves right, to cross the Devonport Leat again, then bears left to head up to a crossroads of tracks on top of a low ridge **H**.

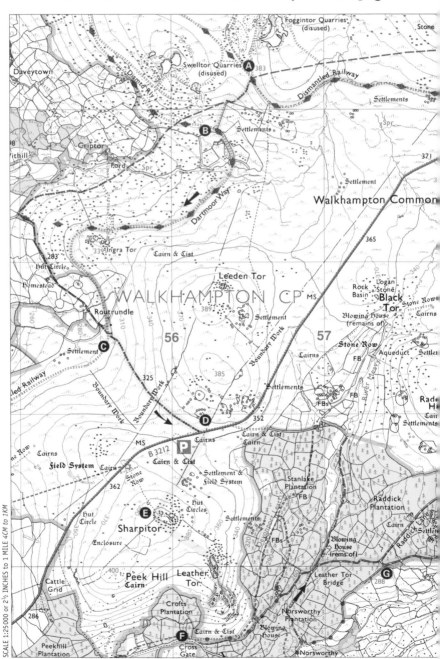

Turn left to go along a clear track across the moor back to Princetown, an easy and relaxing finale to the walk. On the horizon directly ahead is the television mast on North Hessary Tor. Later keep by a wall on the right and continue past South Hessary Tor eventually to reach a gate. Princetown and the forbidding-looking prison are immediately in front. Go through the gate, continue gently downhill along a broad, walled track, go through another gate and keep ahead into Princetown.

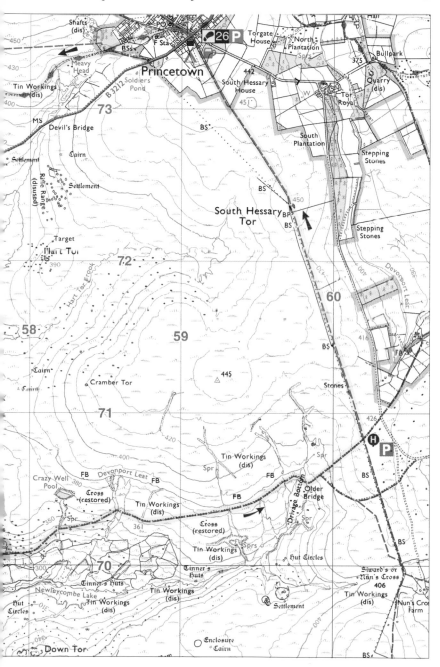

Dittisham, Cornworthy and Tuckenhay

		GPS waypoints
Start	Dittisham. The Ham car park and picnic area beside the River Dart	🖊 SX 864 550
		Ⓐ SX 853 550
Distance	9½ miles (15.25km)	Ⓑ SX 846 551
		Ⓒ SX 831 553
Approximate time	5 hours	Ⓓ SX 829 555
Parking	Dittisham	Ⓔ SX 832 564
Refreshments	Pub at Dittisham, pub at Cornworthy, pub at Tuckenhay	Ⓕ SX 818 560
		Ⓖ SX 816 553
		Ⓗ SX 816 551
Ordnance Survey maps	Landranger 202 (Torbay & South Dartmoor), Explorer OL20 (South Devon)	Ⓙ SX 824 551
		Ⓚ SX 836 544
		Ⓛ SX 842 547
		Ⓜ SX 851 545

This lengthy, varied and energetic route takes you through some of the finest inland scenery in the South Hams. It starts off beside a broad stretch of the River Dart, passes through three attractive and interesting villages, and also takes in farmland, woodland, meadowland and a lovely ramble alongside Bow Creek. This is hilly country and parts of the walk are quite strenuous with a number of steep 'ups and downs'. If the weather is wet there will be muddy tracks and during the summer it is quite likely that some of the field paths will become overgrown. From the higher parts of the walk the views are superb, in particular those overlooking the Dart.

🖊 Start by turning left at the toilet block along the right edge of the recreation area, by a hedge on the right. Bear right on to an enclosed, uphill path and at a T-junction turn right, in the Higher Dittisham direction, to continue uphill, negotiating a mixture of stiles, kissing-gates and steps, eventually bearing left up to a road. Turn right along it into Dittisham, a pleasant village of narrow lanes, old cottages and an impressive 14th- to 15th-century church in a fine position above the River Dart.

At a crossroads in the village centre keep ahead, in the Combe, Cornworthy and Totnes direction, along a lane which bends left and heads downhill to continue beside Dittisham Mill Creek. Turn right Ⓐ, at a public footpath sign, and cross the creek on a wooden footbridge. Continue through a belt of trees to a tarmac track. Cross over, keep ahead up steps to climb a stile and turn left along a path which follows the contours across a sloping field above a stream. At the end of the field continue through an area of scrub to a stile, climb it and walk along an enclosed path, under an avenue of trees, eventually passing through a gate onto a lane. Turn right **B** uphill through the hamlet of East Cornworthy, follow the lane round a left bend and continue steadily uphill. At the top there are grand views across the Dart to the village of Stoke Gabriel on the opposite side.

Descend to a crossroads, turn right **C** downhill along a narrow lane into the quiet and remote village of Cornworthy and at a fork continue down the right-hand lane to pass in front of the attractive, mainly 15th-century church. Almost immediately turn right **D** by the village hall and follow footpath signs through a farmyard. Pass the farmhouse and turn left through two gates between farm buildings and continue downhill along an enclosed track. At the bottom follow a waymark to the left down a pleasant, tree- and hedge-lined track, later keeping along the right edge of a field to the shore of Bow Creek **E**, a delightful spot.

Turn left alongside the creek, climb a stile, walk along the foreshore and the path climbs above the creek. Continue, initially along an enclosed, tree-lined path below wooded slopes – a most attractive part of the walk – later along the bottom edge of a field, and after climbing a stile along a winding, narrow, enclosed path through scrub. Go down steps, walk across a meadow beside the water, cross a footbridge and the path continues into trees to a stile.

Climb this, turn right at a footpath sign a few yards ahead to keep above the creek and follow the path up steps to a waymarked post. Bear right to continue along the bottom edge of a sloping field, and eventually follow the field edge and creek left to a kissing-gate. Pass through and bear first left then right along a narrow path through trees. Descend steps and later the path squeezes between a wire fence on the left and the trees bordering the creek on the right to reach a stone stile. Climb this and turn right over Tuckenhay Bridge to a T-junction.

It is difficult to imagine that in Victorian times this peaceful village was a busy port with warehouses, paper mills, a corn mill, lime kilns and a selection of other industrial enterprises. Tuckenhay was founded in 1806 by the ambitious Abraham Tucker, after whom it was named, but his grandiose plans were later ruined by the silting up of the harbour and nowadays the only reminders of its past activities are the two imposing paper mills at the top end of the village, which have been converted into private apartments.

At the T-junction turn left **F** along

The descent into Cornworthy

a lane, take the first turning on the left (Bridge Terrace), recross the stream and follow the lane to the right and uphill, passing the mill, which closed down in 1917. Continue along a track which heads steeply uphill through woodland and descends to a lane. Turn right, take the first turning on the left **G** to walk along a tarmac track and, by a thatched cottage, turn left **H** along a track to a wooden gate. Go through, continue gently uphill along an enclosed track and pass to the left of barns to go through another wooden gate. Keep along the left edge of a sloping field, by a hedge on the left, as it curves right uphill to a stile in the field corner. Climb this, keep ahead over a footbridge to climb

another, pass a waymarked post and continue uphill, by a line of widely spaced trees on the left, to a waymarked post. Turn right, head across to a stile, climb it and continue along an enclosed path which turns left up to a track. Follow the track to a lane. Turn left, at a fork take the right lane, signposted to Cornworthy, and at a public footpath sign turn right **J** on to a hedge-lined track.

Where the track turns sharp left bear right over a stile; bear left and head gently uphill along the left edge of a field. Go over a stile, continue along the left edge of the next field and cross another stile just before reaching the field corner. Keep along the right edge of the next field and descend steeply to climb a stile. Follow the direction of a waymark diagonally downhill across a field and in the bottom corner bear left

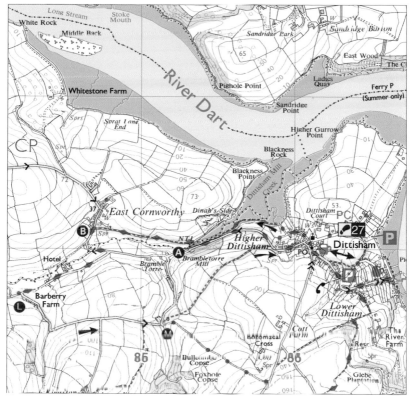

over a stile and footbridge. Bear right and almost immediately left and continue uphill along an enclosed path. At a waymarked post, bear right to continue uphill along the left edge of a field and follow the field edge to the right to climb a stile. Keep along a fenced track with the hedge left and go through a metal gate onto a tarmac lane. Turn left along the lane, which bends left to reach the entrance to Broadridge House. Turn right along a rough, hedge-lined track, heading steeply downhill, and at the bottom cross a stream to another T-junction **K**.

Turn left, beside the stream, on to a pleasant, tree-lined track which ascends gently, curving gradually right, and later descends, equally gently, to a lane **L**. Turn right, in the Kingston direction, along this narrow, winding and undulating lane. Follow

it around a left bend and continue along it for ¾ mile (1.2km) following signs for Dittisham, dropping steeply to where it bends left again. Just round the bend turn right **M** to climb a half-hidden stile to the right of a gate. Turn left and walk between hedges, then keep on in the same direction across a field. Descend into a hollow before climbing again to join the field edge at a corner with a yellow waymark. Follow the right edge of the field uphill to a stile. As you proceed over the brow of the hill, a glorious view unfolds over the Dart valley, one of the finest on the walk.

Climb the stile, head gently downhill to a kissing-gate and then continue down a shady, enclosed track to a lane. Turn right, here rejoining the outward route, into Dittisham and retrace your steps to return to the start.   ●

Buckfastleigh Moor

Start	Holne
Distance	10 miles (16km)
Approximate time	6 hours
Parking	Holne
Refreshments	Pub and café at Holne
Ordnance Survey maps	Landranger 202 (Torbay & South Dartmoor), Explorer OL28 (Dartmoor)

GPS waypoints

- ⬛ SX 706 694
- Ⓐ SX 702 688
- Ⓑ SX 696 689
- Ⓒ SX 687 690
- Ⓓ SX 668 698
- Ⓔ SX 659 690
- Ⓕ SX 668 682
- Ⓖ SX 672 673
- Ⓗ SX 685 659
- Ⓙ SX 698 668
- Ⓚ SX 701 674
- Ⓛ SX 708 679
- Ⓜ SX 710 681
- Ⓝ SX 707 686

At the beginning and end the route follows lanes and tracks, but the remainder of the walk is across the open – and in parts pathless – expanses of Buckfastleigh Moor. This is a long and quite demanding walk with a lot of rough going and boggy conditions can be expected after rain. Because much of it is across rather featureless moorland where the tracks are non-existent and landmarks are few, on no account should this route be attempted in misty conditions by inexperienced walkers; even those who are able to navigate using a compass could well find the section between Ⓓ and Ⓔ difficult. *On a fine day, however, this is a most invigorating walk with a great feeling of spaciousness and freedom, and offering superb and extensive views, especially along the crest of the low ridge from Ryder's Hill, over Snowdon and Pupers Hill to Water Oak Corner. Remember to leave some reserves of energy for the final, steep ¹/₂ mile (800m) pull back up to Holne.*

There is an off-the-beaten-track feel to Holne, tucked away amongst quiet side lanes, but its photogenic cottages, inn and medieval church make it one of the most charming of Dartmoor villages.

🔊 Turn left out of the car park along the lane. At a right-hand bend turn left again, in the Scorriton direction, and head downhill. The lane bends right and continues steeply down through the hamlet of Littlecombe to a left-hand bend Ⓐ.

Take the right lane, follow it for ¹/₂ mile (800m) into Michelcombe and, at another T-junction, turn left Ⓑ along a lane signposted 'No Through Road, Bridleway Only'. Where the lane ends, keep ahead between gateposts, at a sign 'Bridlepath to the Moor', and continue steeply uphill along a sunken, enclosed, hedge-lined track which leads through a metal gate Ⓒ on to the open expanses of Buckfastleigh Moor. Keep ahead along a wide, grassy track, faint but discernible, called the Sandy Way, passing to the right of the first tree that you see and continuing steadily uphill. From now on the views all around are superb. Keep on in a north-westerly direction, crossing a stone footbridge over a leat and passing some stunted trees. As you ascend, the grassy track becomes clearer for a while, cutting a broad swathe through bracken, gorse and heather, and keeping in a north-westerly and later westerly direction.

Head up towards Holne Ridge, passing several stone posts with 'PUDC' inscribed on them. Venford Reservoir can be seen below on the right. Towards the top of the ridge bear left on a grassy track **D** in a south-westerly direction and head across rough, grassy and often boggy moorland to Ryder's Hill. This can be difficult as there is no line of path and no obvious landmarks, apart from a worn track ahead that can be seen heading gently up to the top of the rise. After reaching this track, the vital landmark to make for is the triangulation pillar, and the standing stone beside it, on the 515m (1690ft) summit of Ryder's Hill **E**. The name of the stone, Petre's Bound Stone, indicates that it formerly marked the boundary of an estate. This is a magnificent vantage point over the empty, wild moor and in fine weather the view southwards extends across the South Hams to the coast.

From now on route-finding becomes much easier. The next section is particularly exhilarating as you turn left and head in a south-easterly direction along the broad crest of the ridge, making for a cairn on the next hill, which though called Snowdon bears little resemblance to its more distinguished Welsh namesake. There is a discernible

Trees are a rarity on Buckfastleigh Moor

grassy track in places but conditions underfoot are likely to be soggy. From the cairn **F** continue in the same direction along a gently undulating route, passing a second cairn about 100 yds (91m) farther on, to the rocks and cairn on Pupers Hill **G**, another grand viewpoint. Over to the left the tower of Buckfast Abbey is visible.

From here descend gradually on what is now a good, clear path, heading south-east crossing a grassy track, the Two Moors Way, and soon Avon Dam Reservoir comes into view on the right. Finally the path bears left, towards Water Oak Corner, marked by a small, isolated group of trees dominated by a tall pine, which will have been in sight for some time. Just before reaching the trees turn left **H**, at a crossing of paths, on to the Abbot's Way and then head down to go through a gate, leaving behind the open moor.

Follow a series of waymarked posts across rough pasture, descend to ford a stream and bear left across a field, above and parallel to the stream, to a stile. Climb this, keep ahead to go through a gap in a low hedgebank and continue across several fields, more or less in a straight line, eventually descending towards woodland. The path winds through

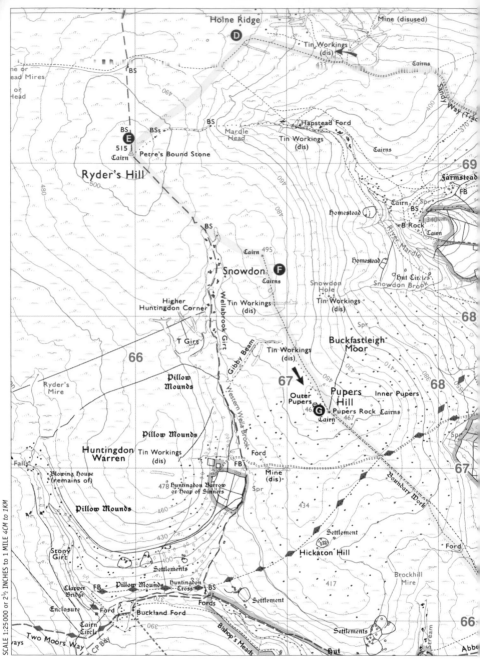

the trees to a signpost, keep ahead through a gate, in the Cross Furzes direction, cross a clapper bridge over the stream and head up an enclosed track to a lane. Turn left, in the Combe and Scorriton direction, and at a junction at Cross Furzes **J** go along the right-hand lane which later descends quite steeply. Where the lane starts to bend slightly left, bear slightly right **K** on a tarmac track. Just before a metal gate, bear left steeply downhill along an enclosed,

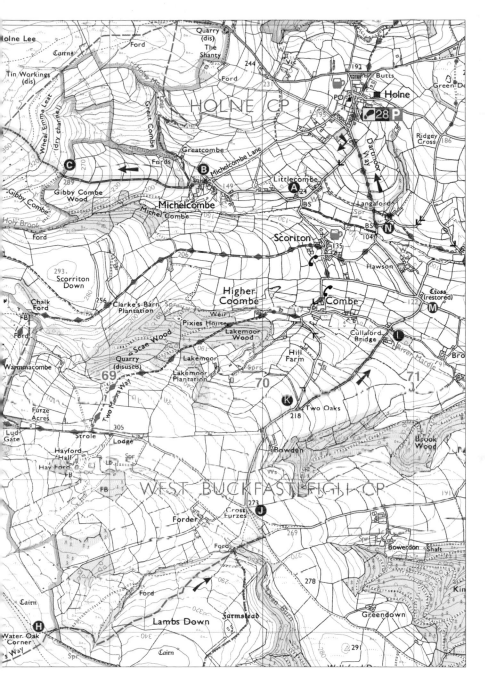

sunken, stony track – this could be muddy – to Cullaford Bridge.

Cross the bridge over the River Mardle ⒧ and continue along the uphill lane ahead to a T-junction by a cross. Turn left ⓜ, in the Holne and Michelcombe direction, and at the three-way junction ahead take the middle lane, signposted to Holne. The lane descends and where it bends right at the bottom, keep ahead ⓝ, at an 'Unsuitable for Motors' sign, along a steep, hedge-lined track for a final, tiring ½ mile (800m) climb. On joining a lane keep ahead into the village of Holne. ●

Further Information

■ The National Parks and Countryside Recreation

Ten National Parks were created in England and Wales as a result of an Act of Parliament in 1949. In addition to these, there are numerous specially designated Areas of Outstanding Natural Beauty, Country and Regional Parks, Sites of Special Scientific Interest and picnic areas scattered throughout England, Wales and Scotland, all of which share the twin aims of preservation of the countryside and public accessibility and enjoyment.

It was after World War II that calls for countryside conservation and access came to fruition in parliament. The National Parks and Countryside Act of 1949 provided for the designation and preservation of areas both of great scenic beauty and of particular wildlife and scientific interest throughout Britain. More specifically it provided for the creation of National Parks in England and Wales. Scotland was excluded at the time because, with greater areas of open space and a smaller population, there were fewer pressures on the Scottish countryside.

A National Parks Commission, a forerunner of the Countryside Commission, was set up, and over the next eight years ten areas were designated as parks; seven in England (Northumberland, Lake District, North York Moors, Yorkshire Dales, Peak District, Exmoor and Dartmoor) and three in Wales (Snowdonia, Brecon Beacons and Pembrokeshire Coast). In 1989 the Norfolk and Suffolk Broads were added to the list; Loch Lomond and the Trossachs followed in 2002, with the Cairngorms in 2003 and the New Forest in 2005. At the same time the Commission was also given the responsibility for designating other smaller areas of high recreational and scenic qualities (Areas of Outstanding Natural Beauty), plus the power to propose and develop long-distance footpaths, now called National Trails.

The authorities who administer the individual National Parks have the very difficult task of reconciling the interests of the people who live and earn their living within them with those of visitors. National Parks are not living museums and there is pressure to exploit the resources of the area, through more intensive farming, or through increased quarrying and forestry, extraction of minerals or the construction of reservoirs.

In the end it all comes down to a question of balance – between conservation and 'sensitive development'. On the one hand there is a responsibility to preserve the natural beauty of the National Parks and to promote their enjoyment by the public, and on the other, the needs and well-being of the people living and working in them have to be borne in mind.

The National Trust

Anyone who likes visiting places of natural beauty and/or historic interest has cause to be grateful to the National Trust. Without it, many such places would probably have vanished by now.

It was in response to the pressures on the countryside posed by the relentless march of Victorian industrialisation that the trust was set up in 1895.

The purpose of the National Trust is to preserve areas of natural beauty and sites of historic interest by acquisition, holding them in trust for the nation and making them available for public access and enjoyment. Some of its properties have been acquired through purchase, but many have been donated. Nowadays it is not only one of the biggest landowners in the country, but also one of the most active conservation charities, protecting well over half a million acres of land, including over 500 miles of coastline and a large number of historic properties in England, Wales and Northern Ireland. (There is a separate

National Trust for Scotland, which was set up in 1931.)

Furthermore, once a piece of land has come under National Trust ownership, it is difficult for its status to be altered. As a result of parliamentary legislation in 1907, the trust was given the right to declare its property inalienable, so ensuring that in any dispute it can appeal directly to parliament.

As it works towards its dual aims of conserving areas of attractive countryside and encouraging greater public access (not easy to reconcile in this age of mass tourism), the trust provides an excellent service to walkers by creating new concessionary paths and waymarked trails, by maintaining stiles and foot bridges and by combating the ever-increasing problem of footpath erosion.

For details of membership, contact the National Trust at the address on page 95.

The Ramblers' Association

No organisation works more actively to protect and extend the rights and interests of walkers in the countryside than the Ramblers' Association. Its aims are clear: to foster a greater knowledge, love and care of the countryside; to assist in the protection and enhancement of public rights of way and areas of natural beauty; to work for greater public access to the countryside; and to encourage more people to take up rambling as a healthy, recreational leisure activity.

It was founded in 1935 when, following the setting up of a National Council of Ramblers' Federation in 1931, a number of federations in London, Manchester, the Midlands and elsewhere came together to create a more effective pressure group, to deal with such problems as the disappearance or obstruction of footpaths, the prevention of access to open mountain and moorland, and increasing hostility from landowners. This was the era of the mass trespasses, when there were sometimes violent confrontations between ramblers and gamekeepers, especially on the moorlands of the Peak District.

Since then the Ramblers' Association has played a key role in preserving and developing the national footpath network, supporting the creation of national parks and encouraging the designation and waymarking of long-distance routes.

Our freedom of access to the countryside, now enshrined in legislation, is still in its early years and requires constant vigilance. But over and above this there will always be the problem of footpaths being illegally obstructed, disappearing through lack of use, or being extinguished by housing or road construction.

It is to meet such problems and dangers that the Ramblers' Association exists and represents the interests of all walkers. The address to write to for information on the Ramblers' Association and how to become a member is given on page 95.

Walkers and the Law

The *Countryside and Rights of Way Act (CRoW Act 2000)* extends the rights of access previously enjoyed by walkers in England and Wales. Implementation of these rights began on 19 September 2004. The Act amends existing legislation and for the first time provides access on foot to certain types of land – defined as mountain, moor, heath, down and registered common land.

Where You Can Go
Rights of Way
Prior to the introduction of the CRoW Act, walkers could only legally access the countryside along public rights of way. These are either 'footpaths' (for walkers only) or 'bridleways' (for walkers, riders on horseback and pedal cyclists). A third category called 'Byways open to all traffic' (BOATs), is used by motorised vehicles as well as those using non-mechanised transport. Mainly they are green lanes, farm and estate roads, although occasionally they will be found crossing mountainous area.

Rights of way are marked on Ordnance Survey maps. Look for the green broken lines on the Explorer maps, or the red dashed lines on Landranger maps.

The term 'right of way' means exactly what it says. It gives a right of passage over what, for the most part, is private land. Under pre-CRoW legislation walkers were required to keep to the line of the right of way and not stray onto land on either side. If you did inadvertently wander off the right of way, either because of faulty map reading or because the route was not clearly indicated on the ground, you were technically trespassing.

Local authorities have a legal obligation to ensure that rights of way are kept clear and free of obstruction, and are signposted where they leave metalled roads. The duty of local authorities to install signposts extends to the placing of signs along a path or way, but only where the authority considers it necessary to have a signpost or waymark to assist persons unfamiliar with the locality.

The New Access Rights
Access Land

As well as being able to walk on existing rights of way, under the new legislation you now have access to large areas of open land. You can of course continue to use rights of way footpaths to cross this land, but the main difference is that you can now lawfully leave the path and wander at will, but only in areas designated as access land.

Where to Walk

Areas now covered by the new access rights – Access Land – are shown on Ordnance Survey Explorer maps bearing the access land symbol on the front cover.

'Access Land' is shown on Ordnance Survey maps by a light yellow tint surrounded by a pale orange border. New orange coloured 'i' symbols on the maps will show the location of permanent access information boards installed by the access authorities.

Restrictions

The right to walk on access land may lawfully be restricted by landowners.

Landowners can, for any reason, restrict access for up to 28 days in any year. They cannot however close the land:
- on bank holidays;
- for more than four Saturdays and Sundays in a year;
- on any Saturday from 1 June to 11 August; or
- on any Sunday from 1 June to the end of September.

They have to provide local authorities with five working days' notice before the date of closure unless the land involved is an area of less than five hectares or the closure is for less than four hours. In these cases landowners only need to provide two hours' notice.

Whatever restrictions are put into place on access land they have no effect on existing rights of way, and you can continue to walk on them.

Dogs

Dogs can be taken on access land, but must be kept on leads of two metres or less between 1 March and 31 July, and at all times where they are near livestock. In addition landowners may impose a ban on all dogs from fields where lambing takes place for up to six weeks in any year. Dogs may be banned from moorland used for grouse shooting and breeding for up to five years.

In the main, walkers following the routes in this book will continue to follow existing rights of way, but a knowledge and understanding of the law as it affects walkers, plus the ability to distinguish access land marked on the maps, will enable anyone who wishes to depart from paths that cross access land either to take a shortcut, to enjoy a view or to explore.

General Obstructions

Obstructions can sometimes cause a problem on a walk and the most common of these is where the path across a field has been ploughed over. It is legal for a farmer to plough up a path provided that it is restored within two weeks. This does not always happen and you are faced with the

Countryside Access Charter

Your rights of way are:

- public footpaths – on foot only. Sometimes waymarked in yellow
- bridleways – on foot, horseback and pedal cycle. Sometimes waymarked in blue
- byways (usually old roads), most 'roads used as public paths' and, of course, public roads – all traffic has the right of way

Use maps, signs and waymarks to check rights of way. Ordnance Survey Explorer and Landranger maps show most public rights of way

On rights of way you can:

- take a pram, pushchair or wheelchair if practicable
- take a dog (on a lead or under close control)
- take a short route round an illegal obstruction or remove it sufficiently to get past

You have a right to go for recreation to:

- public parks and open spaces – on foot
- most commons near older towns and cities – on foot and sometimes on horseback
- private land where the owner has a formal agreement with the local authority

In addition you can use the following by local or established custom or consent, but ask for advice if you are unsure:

- many areas of open country, such as moorland, fell and coastal areas, especially those in the care of the National Trust, and some commons
- some woods and forests, especially those owned by the Forestry Commission
- country parks and picnic sites
- most beaches
- canal towpaths
- some private paths and tracks Consent sometimes extends to horse-riding and cycling

For your information:

- county councils and London boroughs maintain and record rights of way, and register commons
- obstructions, dangerous animals, harassment and misleading signs on rights of way are illegal and you should report them to the county council
- paths across fields can be ploughed, but must normally be reinstated within two weeks
- landowners can require you to leave land to which you have no right of access
- motor vehicles are normally permitted only on roads, byways and some 'roads used as public paths'

---

dilemma of following the line of the path, even if this means treading on crops, or walking round the edge of the field. Although the later course of action seems the most sensible, it does mean that you would be trespassing.

Other obstructions can vary from overhanging vegetation to wire fences across the path, locked gates or even a cattle feeder on the path.

Use common sense. If you can get round the obstruction without causing damage, do so. Otherwise only remove as much of the obstruction as is necessary to secure passage.

If the right of way is blocked and cannot be followed, there is a long-standing view that in such circumstances there is a right

to deviate, but this cannot wholly be relied on. Although it is accepted in law that highways (and that includes rights of way) are for the public service, and if the usual track is impassable, it is for the general good that people should be entitled to pass into another line. However, this should not be taken as indicating a right to deviate whenever a way becomes impassable. If in doubt, retreat.

Report obstructions to the local authority and/or the Ramblers' Association.

Global Positioning System (GPS)

What is GPS?
GPS is a worldwide radio navigation system that uses a network of 24 satellites

and receivers, usually hand-held, to calculate positions. By measuring the time it takes a signal to reach the receiver, the distance from the satellite can be estimated. Repeat this with several satellites and the receiver can then use triangulation to establish the position of the receiver.

How to use GPS with Ordnance Survey mapping

Each of the walks in this book includes GPS co-ordinate data that reflects the walk position points on Ordnance Survey maps.

GPS and OS maps use different models for the earth and co-ordinate systems, so when you are trying to relate your GPS position to features on the map the two will differ slightly. This is especially the case with height, as the model that relates the GPS global co-ordinate system to height above sea level is very poor.

When using GPS with OS mapping, some distortion – up to 16ft (5m) – will always be present. Moreover, individual features on maps may have been surveyed only to an accuracy of 23ft (7m) (for 1:25000 scale maps), while other features, e.g. boulders, are usually only shown schematically.

In practice, this should not cause undue difficulty, as you will be near enough to your objective to be able to spot it.

How to use the GPS data in this book

There are various ways you can use the GPS data in this book.

1. Follow the route description while checking your position on your receiver when you are approaching a position point.

2. You can also use the positioning information on your receiver to verify where you are on the map.

3. Alternatively, you can use some of the proprietary software that is available. At the simple end there is inexpensive software, which lets you input the walk positions (waypoints), download them to the gps unit and then use them to assist your navigation on the walks.

At the upper end of the market Ordnance Survey maps are available in electronic form. Most come with software that enables you to enter your walking route onto the map, download it to your gps unit and use it, alongside the route description, to follow the route.

 ## Useful Organisations

Campaign to Protect Rural England
128 Southwark Street,
London SE1 0SW
Tel. 020 7981 2800
www.cpre.org.uk

Council for National Parks
6/7 Barnard Mews,
London SW11 1QU
Tel. 020 7924 4077
www.cnp.org.uk

Dartmoor National Park Authority (DNPA)
Parke, Bovey Tracey, Newton Abbot,
Devon TQ13 9JQ
Tel: 01626 832093
www.dartmoor-npa.gov.uk
See also
www.virtuallydartmoor.org.uk
National Park Visitor Centres:
Haytor: 01364 661520
New Bridge: 01364 631303
Postbridge: 01822 880272
Princetown, The High Moorland Visitor Centre: 01822 890414
Local DNPA information points:
Belstone, The Tors
Chagford, Courtyard Café
Christow post office
Drewsteignton post office
Horrabridge, Summerfield newsagent
Lydford petrol station
Meavy, The Royal Oak pub
Sticklepath, Sticklepath Stores
Widecombe, Sexton's Cottage (NT shop)
Yelverton petrol station

Forestry Commission England
Great Eastern House,
Tenison Road, Cambridge
CB1 2DU

Tel: 01223 314546
www.forestry.gov.uk

National Trust
Membership and general enquiries:
PO Box 39, Warrington
WA5 7WD
Tel: 0870 458 4000
www.nationaltrust.org.uk
Devon
Killerton House, Broadclyst,
Exeter EX5 3LE
Tel. 01392 881691

Natural England
Level 2, Renslade House,
Bonhay Road, Exeter EX4 3AW
Tel: 01392 889770

Ordnance Survey
Romsey Road, Southampton
SO16 4GU
Tel. 08456 050505
www.ordnancesurvey.co.uk

Ramblers' Association
87–90 Albert Embankment,
London SE1 7TW
Tel. 020 7339 8500
www.ramblers.org.uk

South West Tourism
Woodwater Park, Exeter EX2 5WT
Tel. 01392 360050
www.swtourism.co.uk

Tourist information centres (South Devon):
Axminster: 01297 34386
Brixham: 01803 852861
Budleigh Salterton: 01395 445275
Dartmouth: 01803 834224
Dawlish: 01626 215665
Exeter: 01392 265700
Exmouth: 01395 222299
Honiton: 01404 43716
Kingsbridge: 01548 853195
Newton Abbot: 01626 215667
Ottery St Mary: 01404 813964
Paignton: 01803 558383
Plymouth: 01752 306330
Salcombe: 01548 843927
Seaton: 01297 21660
Sidmouth: 01395 516441

Teignmouth: 01626 215666
Torquay: 01803 296296
Totnes: 01803 863168
Tourist information centres (Dartmoor):
Okehampton: 01837 53020
Tavistock: 01822 612938
Community information centres (Dartmoor):
Ashburton: 01364 653426
Bovey Tracey: 01626 832047
Buckfastleigh: 01364 644522
Ivybridge: 01752 897035
Moretonhampstead: 01647 440043

 Ordnance Survey maps of South Devon and Dartmoor

The walks described in this guide are covered by Ordnance Survey 1:50 000 scale (1¼ inches to 1 mile or 2cm to 1km) Landranger map sheets 191, 192, 201, 202. These all-purpose maps are packed with information to help you explore the area. Viewpoints, picnic sites, places of interest and caravan and camping sites are shown, as well as public rights of way information such as footpaths and bridleways.

To examine the area in more detail, and especially if you are planning walks, the Ordnance Survey Explorer maps at 1:25 000 scale (2½ inches to 1 mile or 4cm to 1km) are ideal. Maps covering the area are:

OL20 (South Devon)
OL28 (Dartmoor)
110 (Torquay & Dawlish)
114 (Exeter & the Exe Valley)
115 (Exmouth & Sidmouth)
116 (Lyme Regis & Bridport)

To get to South Devon and Dartmoor use the Ordnance Survey OS Travel Map-Route Great Britain at 1:625 000 (4cm to 25km or 1 inch to 10 miles) scale or OS Travel Map-Road 7 (South West England and South Wales) at 1:250 000 (1cm to 2.5km or 1 inch to 4 miles) scale.

Ordnance Survey maps and guides are available from most booksellers, stationers and newsagents.